# SACRED SPACE

## Embraced with Love, Mercy, and Grace

### Linda L. Goodwin

Copyright © 2018 by Linda L. Goodwin.

All rights reserved. This book or any portion thereof may not be reproduced or used in any manner whatsoever without the express written permission of the publisher except for the use of brief quotations in a book review.

Publishing Services provided by Paper Raven Books

Printed in the United States of America

First Printing, 2018

Paperback ISBN= 978-1-7326063-0-2
Hardback ISBN= 978-1-7326063-1-9

In Memory of

*Diane "Tootie" Allison*

Your beautiful smile and delightful presence
are greatly missed by your family and friends.

AND

Dedicated to

*Chaplains*

serving vital ministries in their unique communities.

*Listen to your life. See it for the fathomless mystery that it is. In the boredom and pain of it no less than in the excitement and gladness: touch, taste, smell your way to the holy and hidden heart of it because in the last analysis all moments are key moments, and life itself is grace.*
—Frederick Buechner, American Theologian and Writer, *Listening to Your Life: Daily Meditations*

# Table Of Contents

| | |
|---|---:|
| Foreword | 1 |
| Introduction | 3 |
| Chapter 1: Pathway to Adventure | 7 |
| Chapter 2: Pathway to Sacred Space | 19 |
| Chapter 3: Pathway to Intimacy with God | 27 |
| Chapter 4: Pathway to Spiritual Growth | 39 |
| Chapter 5: Pathway of Struggle | 51 |
| Chapter 6: Pathway to Chaplaincy | 61 |
| Chapter 7: Pathway to Clinical Pastoral Education | 69 |
| Chapter 8: Pathway to Pediatric Chaplaincy | 75 |
| Chapter 9: Pathway of Sorrow | 85 |
| Chapter 10: Pathway to Healing | 105 |
| Chapter 11: Pathway to Transformation | 119 |
| Acknowledgements | 133 |
| Bibliography | 135 |
| Suicide & Grief Resources | 139 |
| Additional Resources | 143 |

# Foreword

We live in an era of material success. But it is not delivering on its promises. The business motivations of competition and productivity have left many feeling alone. We have exchanged career for vocation, success for integrity, and doing for being. Roles we aspire to prove unrewarding in any meaningful way. Constant entertainment, while titillating, has not proven fulfilling. Addictions to alcohol, drugs, food, TV, video games are meant to assuage our unnamed pains, but fail. Betrayal by social structures like government and religion has left us adrift and bereft.

So it is not surprising many people are turning to spirituality, looking for a sense of comfort and hope. Linda's book is about one such journey, her struggle with acknowledging, developing, and nurturing a relationship with God. I think the richness of the book is in its honesty. You can see this in her use of traditional religious ideas but also in her descriptions of the adventure. She does not sugarcoat the difficulties of life nor the struggles of pursuing the spiritual life. Yet she affirms the joys experienced and thrill of living in God's love, mercy, and grace. Behind her journey is Christ's model of the inexplicable connection between death and resurrection. Death or loss is inevitable, sometimes even chosen, and it provides a fertile bed for the growth of the unexpected. By sharing her confusion, grief, frustration, and brokenness in God's presence, Linda makes the wonder, awe, and grace palpable. As such, it is a realistic view of the spiritual life, to which we are all invited.

Linda offers ways she has found helpful to cherishing your relationship with God and heeding his call to your vocation.

I hope you find some of them helpful, too. While her path led to ordained ministry and pediatric chaplaincy, your path will be unique to you. Hopefully, you will find her examples apt for your own lives. Finding ways to incorporate God into all aspects of your life will take you into unexplored territory. Past experiences you had, but failed to reflect upon, will offer up new gifts. God will invite you into pathways you never thought you would take, accompanied by serenity and joy.

But it is important to remember each of us is unique, we have a unique relationship with God and a unique vocation to discover. So it is not as important to copy Linda's methods as to emulate her tenacity to stay on the adventure. The spiritual life is not a procedure, but a process, or in Linda's words an "adventure," which by its very definition is unpredictable. I hope reading Linda's book gives you suggestions, encouragement, and hope on discovering your own pathway.

> Paul Derrickson
> M.Div., APC Certified Chaplain, ACPE Clinical Educator (retired)
> August 19, 2018

# Introduction

Each story, yours and mine, has the power to influence and inspire others in their own life's journey. All of our life experiences mold and shape us into unique human beings. By respecting and honoring our stories and the stories of others, and by sharing our own vulnerabilities, we can offer encouragement and inspire others to be empowered, especially in times of adversity. My story was written from a series of journal entries. It is one of overcoming personal and spiritual struggles as I faced difficult times: an unexpected and painful path towards divorce, leaving my home and loved ones for a new calling, supporting families in my work as a pediatric chaplain, and the loss of my husband to suicide. All of these times in my life served as important milestones on my spiritual adventure and have deepened my relationship with God.

Throughout this book, I will weave my story with a sampling of spiritual disciplines that I integrated into my personal daily devotions and further enriched my contemplative practice. I begin by introducing and defining spiritual adventure and sacred space, which are the cornerstones of my journey. Spiritual adventure is an attitude that enables us to better understand our life's journey to discover meaning for our lives and begins with recognizing and responding to God. Sacred space is an awareness of and attentiveness to the presence of the Holy within a designated and blessed space. It is a unique place that feels separated from real time and allows you to enter into God's time. As a chaplain, I have found sacred space in times when people share their stories of painful struggle. It is within the context of deep and vulnerable sharing that a chaplain brings a sense of God's presence and embrace of love, mercy, and grace.

Throughout this book, I also share a deeply personal account of my flawed attempt to salvage my marriage through my prayer time with God, which then led to my discernment process for something more meaningful in ministry. That process took me to a Clinical Pastoral Education assignment for 15 months at Penn State Hershey Medical Center and later led me to the pediatric chaplain position there. One of the darkest times of my life was when my husband, Russ, died from suicide, and it has taken me over eight years to be able to write or speak about this loss. The complicated grief that suicide loss survivors struggle with, heightened by the stigma and shame of suicide, brings to light the challenges facing our faith communities to provide a new theological framework of suicide and to support families facing the loss of a loved one to suicide.

At the end of each chapter, I hope you will receive the reflection questions as an opportunity for journaling and contemplation of the mystery of the Divine. Each chapter closes with a blessing, which reflects a practice I began as a hospital chaplain. Oftentimes during a visit with a patient, I realized they were uncomfortable with a formal prayer but were accepting and encouraged by words of blessing. I hope my words of affirmation for your uniqueness and value as a child of God resonate with you and bring you comfort.

I will end with the same premise I begin with: our personal devotional time with God can assist us in our faith journey as we listen to God in prayer, guided by the Scriptures and other practices to enable us to hear and obey God's voice.[1]

---

1 All Bible references are from the New Revised Standard Version unless otherwise indicated.

*Introduction*

Understanding that God will never abandon us, we continue the pathway to discover our purpose for life, that unknown destination that offers new possibilities and a future with hope.

Grace and peace to you in your own spiritual adventure. May God open the eyes of your spiritual heart to see beyond the limits you have set for yourself, to the hope of new possibilities that God has for you.

# CHAPTER 1
## PATHWAY TO ADVENTURE

*Spiritual Adventure*

> *For surely I know the plans I have for you, says the Lord, plans for your welfare and not for harm, to give you a future with hope.*
> —Jeremiah 29:11

While driving to work one fall morning, as I rounded a sharp bend with the steep hillside on my left and a sharp drop from the guardrails on the right, I took my hands off the steering wheel and raised them in the air as I said, "Yes, Lord, I'll do it, I'll go!" This moment was a culmination of over a year of seeking God's insight and understanding. I had been searching for *something more* for my ministry and for my life. This was my moment of surrender, a response unlike any other, a yielding that resulted from my fervent desire to follow God's leading after a period of spiritual discernment.

When I began my discernment process, I could not perceive any possibilities for anything new and exciting that existed beyond my own personal and professional limitations. Throughout this process, however, I maintained a willingness to engage with God. It became an adventure as I devoted myself to increasing my attentiveness to the Divine by listening more fully. I structured my personal devotions to read, pray, and journal the Scriptures with a trust that God would lead to new possibilities and a new future with hope.

How was I able to get to this point in my life where my faith and trust in God enabled me to respond in this manner? First, my daily devotions for many years had established a foundation of study, contemplation, and listening for God in the Scriptures as well as in daily living. Second, I had engaged in studying the various spiritual disciplines and had integrated several practices into my devotional time. The third and most significant influence that enabled me to yield to God was confronting the struggles in my faith and my life. Those personal and spiritual challenges were what informed and transformed my relationship and trust in God. Those painful struggles were pivotal in strengthening my faith and empowering me to say, "Yes, Lord, I'll do it. I'll go!" In my obedience, I was liberated and enabled to move from a static place of limitations onto a pathway of possibilities that inspired hope.

There are significant aspects to consider when we are at the crossroads of decision-making. It is God who awaits our invitation to be a part of our discernment process. And God enables us to see beyond our limitations and past the boundaries we have established for ourselves. It is with God's participation in discernment that new possibilities are revealed, new opportunities that we never considered attainable.

In 2006, I was at such a crossroad. At that time, I was already invested in a fulfilling 14-year ministry that enabled me to explore and develop my spiritual gifts in creative ways. Some of my responsibilities included providing resources to pastors and congregations, organizing learning events and retreats, and leading youth ministry. I found the position both challenging and enjoyable. At some point, though, I recognized a growing dissatisfaction in my spirit, and I began to feel that I no longer fit in that particular role. Simultaneously, my personal life and struggles with my marriage forced me to focus on God's leading in my devotional time. My spiritual heart, that place that is attuned to listening for God, desired something more. I asked for God's guidance as I initiated my discernment.

It was with a spirit of adventure that I began this process. By May of 2007, I responded fully to God's call, which resulted in leaving my family and friends at home and parting ways from a very supportive ministry and community. As a new season of my life began, away from those intangibles of comfort and security, I had no idea that by trusting in God I would discover my calling as a pediatric chaplain. By leaving all that was familiar and moving into an uncertain future, I embraced my adventure with God.

The term "adventure" captures a distinctive attitude that embodies dynamic energy to live courageously and boldly with passion as we engage with God in a search for meaning and purpose. These principles are based on the premise that spirit of adventure begins through recognizing God's love for us as we engage in a relationship with God and commit to Christ as the foundation of our faith. Once established, this relationship is nurtured by personal devotions of Scripture reading and prayer. When engaging in the spirit of adventure, we experience spiritual growth as well as spiritual resiliency, the stamina needed to face adversity. Throughout this adventure, we engage in a discovery of new pockets of our inner self, the many unexplored facets that are intertwined throughout our faith and our lives. By acknowledging these principles and crossing the threshold into a new spiritual pathway, we are accepting God's invitation to personal discovery and empowerment.

In the book *Adventure in Everything* by Matthew Walker, the author breaks down the definition of adventure into five elements: 1) High Endeavor, the ability to think big about who you are, how you live, and what you can do in the world; 2) Total Commitment, the spirit of willingness to embrace a challenge with confidence and belief; 3) Uncertain Outcome, the acknowledgement that a predetermined outcome is not adventure; 4) Tolerance for Adversity, the capacity to be resilient in the face of challenge; and 5) Great Companionship, the understanding that we can't do this alone.[2]

Putting these essential elements into a Christian framework gives a basis for defining spiritual adventure.

> Adventure awaits us as God calls us to Divine Love through our relationship and commitment to Christ. It is with an open heart and an awareness of the Holy Spirit's guidance that we pray and contemplate the Scriptures as a vital means of *listening*. It is in our *obedience* that we bravely explore the path we are called to, which is an uncertain destination. *Trusting* that God is with us and will not abandon us, we are enabled to confront any adversity we may encounter. With determination, we embrace this challenge as we welcome new possibilities and a new future with hope.

This definition should be fluid as it continues to resonate and evolve through each individual's own experiences with God. It is a starting point that allows us to explore and define our own adventure.

> *I therefore, the prisoner in the Lord, beg you to lead a life worthy of the calling to which you have been called, with all humility and gentleness, with patience, bearing with one another in love.*
> —Ephesians 4:1–2

---

2 Walker, Matthew. Adventure in Everything: *How the Five Elements of Adventure Create a Life of Authenticity, Purpose, and Inspiration.* New York: Hay House, Inc., 2011.

The word adventure inspires thoughts of superheroes and battles. The Scripture is alive with stories that depict the many people of faith who had remarkable adventures. What we must realize, though, is that these Bible illustrations were about ordinary, flawed individuals who demonstrated extraordinary faith and trust in God. They listened, responded with obedience, and trusted God in their situations. Abraham, favored by God, packed up his household and left his homeland to travel through unknown territories and dangers to an uncertain destination. Moses, a conduit for a series of devastating plagues, led the Israelites out of bondage. Elijah, the beloved prophet and miracle worker, responded to God and was then taken into heaven by a chariot and horses of fire. Deborah, the only female judge mentioned in the Bible, achieved an important military victory. Esther, the beautiful queen, was a key figure in an intriguing plot that might have resulted in her death. Mary and Martha, two sisters who practiced hospitality, provided a safe haven for Jesus during dangerous times with Martha's practical management skills and Mary's spiritual focus. Paul and the disciples certainly faced danger, hardships, shipwrecks, and jail time as they responded to Christ's call.

These are only a few of many stories that illustrate the risk and uncertainty of adventure. While I am not suggesting that God demands unusual or heroic acts from any one of us, I am proposing that, with God, many things are possible that we cannot even envision. As we take our first step into our adventure, recognize and acknowledge that God calls us into a relationship with him. To begin, we are introduced to Divine Love.

> *For I am the LORD your God, the Holy one of Israel, your Savior. Because you are precious in my sight, and honored, and I love you.*
> —Isaiah 43:3, 4a

**Embrace Love**

There is a place, deep within my heart, that yearns for love. The all-encompassing, far-reaching, and magnificent love that knows me, accepts me unconditionally, and embraces me. God's love is so much more than I have ever known, and words are very imprecise and limiting when I try to explain it. The desire of my heart is to encourage you to believe and experience the embrace of God's love.

We are created in the image of the Divine; thus, every human being is worthy of love, honor, and respect. Genesis 1:26 says, *"God said, 'Let us make humankind in our image, according to our likeness.'"* Divine Love is important to understand as we face life and its obstacles. When overwhelming problems erode and destroy our own self-worth, when we think we are not enough, when we question whether we really have any purpose for living, then God's Divine Love is a necessary foundation, a reminder of our significance. God's indwelling presence can support, strengthen, and show us the meaning of unconditional love, forgiveness, and grace. It is in that place, in your innermost heart, where your spirit recognizes and delights in the realization that you are God's beloved.

This understanding that as God's creation I was worthy of God's unconditional love was the most profound learning of my Christian faith and was an understanding that I lacked in my younger years. The teenage and young adult years are frightening for most of us, especially as we deal with the pressures of making decisions about education, career choices, and relationships. To make matters worse, we are often judged on our appearance and material goods as well as type of jobs and income. We place enormous expectations on ourselves and then label or categorize our worth based on these values. I was no different. As a young adult, I believed the lies and labels and allowed the fear of never being enough to rule my thoughts. It was my own self-rejection that kept me from fully understanding and accepting God's love. It was easier to blame myself than to believe in God's grace. Mistakenly, I believed that my worth was based on my work and responsibilities and believed that my hard work and accomplishments served as a confirmation and validation of my worth.

Distortions of superiority and inferiority are common barriers to accepting God's Divine Love, and our world continues to perpetuate those distortions. Romans 12:3 tells us, *"Do not think of yourselves more highly than you ought to think, but to think with sober judgment."* Humility is not only about not thinking too much of yourself, it is also being fully aware of your significance. As the priest and theologian Henri Nouwen has stated in numerous books, understanding that we are God's *beloved* actually means we have to claim our *belovedness* in Christ Jesus.[3]

---

3 Nouwen, Henri J. M. *Spiritual Direction: Wisdom for the Long Walk of Faith.* New York: HarperCollins, 2006, p. 28.

> *To those who are called, who are beloved in God the Father and kept safe for Jesus Christ.*
> —Jude 1

Embracing our belovedness allows our spiritual heart to begin that first step in relationship with God. The moment I embraced my belovedness was a pivotal moment in my life, a turning away from old understandings and turning in a new direction. This is *metanoia*, a Greek word that means changing one's mind; it is a relinquishment of those lies about our worthiness in moving towards a new love for the Lord. This liberation from the eroding lies frees us from our former understandings of self and invites us to look beyond our thinking and relating to the Lord and the world. A powerful Scripture that addresses this found in Matthew 11:28: *"Come to me, all you that are weary and are carrying heavy burdens, and I will give you rest."* It invites us to be a part of a transformative process, a change of heart, as we respond to the invitation.

Through contemplation and deepening our prayer life, our former way of thinking falls away and we are gradually changed from a person who is fearful to fearless, from a focus on self to selfless, as we live our way into a new creation. It is in that place, in our innermost heart, where our spirit recognizes and delights in the realization that we are God's beloved. We are God's creation, as it says in Genesis 1:26. *"Then God said, 'Let us make humankind in our image, according to our likeness.'"* Since we are created in the image of the Divine, every human being is worthy of honor and respect, worthy of love and significance.

Divine Love is an important understanding for all of us as we face adversity.

As God's blessed children, we are part of the family of believers that should continually offer blessings, words of respect, and honor to each other. The word *namaste* is an ancient Sanskrit greeting still used in India today, a compassionate greeting that honors and respects, encourages and validates. It's similar to hello, but with deep respect implied, and translates to "the divine in me, bows (respects) to the divine in you." To me, this phrase reflects God's indwelling as well as a reflection of Christ's love for us. It's unfortunate that our cultural trends indicate a decline from respect to disrespect as our society moves towards increased objectifying and criticizing others. These types of behavior are cruel and in direct opposition to Christ's example of caring for others. Instead of reacting to an attitude of hostility, we are to reflect Christ's love with kindness and concern. By recognizing that oftentimes it is pain that fuels the hostility in another's heart, we are able to respond with understanding and empathy.

**Reflections**

- What elements of the term "spirit of adventure" speak to you regarding your spiritual growth?

- Have you ever struggled with unworthiness and a fear of never being enough? What can you do to release those lies and acknowledge Divine Love?

- Read John 1:35–39 silently and aloud. Listen for Jesus's voice as he asks you: *What are you looking for?* Journal your reflections.

## Blessing

*May God's light shine upon your path*
*illuminating the way to*
*your own spiritual adventure*
*into the mystery beyond.*

# CHAPTER 2
# PATHWAY TO SACRED SPACE

*Creating Sacred Space*

> *But God, who is rich in mercy, out of great love with which he loved us even when we were dead through our trespasses, made us alive together with Christ—by grace you have been saved.*
> —Ephesians 2:4, 5

What is *sacred space?* It is the time and space designated to awareness of and attentiveness to the presence of the Holy. It is a unique place that feels separated from real time and invites you to enter into God's time. It is a place to encounter and experience the Holy. You create sacred space by identifying a physical place that allows privacy and quiet as well as acknowledging God's presence by prayer. A fundamental element of creating sacred space is to recognize the active participation and guidance of the Divine within the process. This sacred space is often intuitively claimed by chaplains, ministers, and people of faith as they enter into prayer.

There are several ways to utilize sacred space, and two are illustrated in this chapter. The first is to recognize that hospital chaplains introduce shared sacred space as they meet with patients and their families, by bringing an awareness of God's presence in an intentional manner amidst the chaos of life. Love, mercy, and grace are touchstones of the chaplains shared sacred space as they listen and respond to someone's story of a situation or a struggle that weighs heavily on the heart. Within this sharing, God's presence permeates the sacred space to allow the deeply personal, and often painful, revelations to unfold. The faces telling their stories may change, but there are often common themes of unresolved conflict and grief, inability to cope, confusion, and confession. In my experience, there is a fluid ebb and flow of compassion in listening and responding to the emotional and spiritual needs expressed and as Divine Love initiates new perspectives and new possibilities that allows for forgiveness and redemption, healing and hope, wisdom and understanding.

The second illustration is creating a sacred space to establish a personal devotion time to meet with the Divine. In this time, you are able to simply *be* with God, allowing the Holy Spirit, in a wordless and loving manner, to be able to touch and transform your spirit. This setting is created to allow you to be attentive to the Holy Spirit as you develop and deepen intimacy with God. Just as you spend time with a new friend, talking and learning about that person, you must also spend time with God.

In dedicating yourself to being with God in prayer, meditation, and reading the Scriptures, the physical space must allow you to be in a comfortable position with quiet, uninterrupted, and private time. If you have a table available, you can add a candle, an icon, a rosary, prayer beads, or any item that is a reminder of the Holy for you. Your Bible, prayer book, journal, and even a hymnal, if you prefer, could be available.

As you welcome the Divine by invocation or a prayer of invitation, your focus should be on the Holiness of God. With reverence and awe, you prepare to be present with the Lord in your spiritual heart, that place deep in your being that can be filled only by God. It is the place where we harbor and protect the pain and disappointments of life, where our vulnerabilities are known to God. Recognize that the Spirit works deep within our innermost being, so deeply that sometimes we cannot identify its presence. By claiming an intimate relationship with God, we are not passively submitting but actively waiting on God who waits for us.

*Chapter 2: Pathway to Sacred Space*

> *I pray that the God of our Lord Jesus Christ, the Father of glory, may give you a spirit of wisdom and revelation as you come to know him, so that, with the eyes of your heart enlightened, you may know what is the hope to which he has called you.*
> —Ephesians 1:17, 18

**Reverence for Holy God**

Our own attitude should be one of deep respect and honor as we acknowledge the Holiness of God. It is with reverence to God that we come into our relationship, into the sacred space we have claimed. The Scriptures proclaim and revere God using terms such as *awe* and *wonder*. Jewish theologian and philosopher Abraham Joshua Heschel tells us that, "Awe is a sense for the transcendence, for the reference everywhere to Him who is beyond all things."[4] Psalm 33:8 says, *"Let all the earth fear the LORD; let all the inhabitants of the world stand in awe of him."* As we spend more time in God's presence, we begin to recognize and revere the Holiness of our Lord.

Awe moves us into insight and understanding of the omnipotence, the authority, the all-powerfulness of God. The more time we spend in God's presence, the more we realize words are insignificant and are of no consequence in defining awe. Words cannot define the indefinable. Our language limits us in explaining the *awe* of God, because God is ineffable and indescribable. In God's presence, as we experience the *awe* of

---

4 Heschel, Abraham Joshua. God In Search of Man: A Philosophy of Judaism. New York: Farrar, Straus and Giroux, 1955, p. 75.

God, this encourages and enables our insight and understanding to expand. Other words used in Scripture that assist in illustrating the *awe* of God are *fear*, *revere*, and *my heart trembles*. These words and phrases serve as a significant reminder of an important attitude toward our sublime God.

Wonder is a quality that enables us to connect with the Divine, to encourage and renew our own spirit, and to remind us of God's presence in everyday matters. We value the aspect of wonder as we reflect on the Holy, recognizing the beauty of being surprised and inspired by our Creator God: inspired by the splendor of a sunset, surprised by random acts of kindness by strangers, awed by the beauty and grandeur of nature. When we lose touch with our wonder, we have lost an important element of our spirit.

**God Moments**

By attentiveness to the Lord in our devotional time, we begin to recognize God's presence throughout our day, in real time. These God moments are those times when God interrupts our ordinary, everyday lives by breaking through our routine with an unexpected reminder of Presence. These God moments can be startling as well as inspiring. These are moments when the Sacred reminds us that God is not confined nor defined within the boundaries of a worship structure. Indeed, the Sacred surrounds us and only awaits our awareness and our acknowledgment. Awareness to these moments can be cultivated and fine-tuned through intentional time spent being with God. Through our daily devotions and prayer time, we become sensitive to the Presence of Holiness. God moments belong to God. I don't consider them random acts, coincidences, or serendipity. As a Christian, I perceive these interruptions as gentle reminders that God is present and immanent in our everyday living—those moments that warm our heart, lighten our spirit, and remind us of God's love. As I tell you about my work as a pediatric chaplain, I'll explain more about God moments.

> *Open my eyes, so that I may behold wondrous things…*
> —Psalm 119:18

**Reflections**

- What steps would you take to create a sacred space for your daily devotions? Ask God's wisdom as you plan for establishing and continuing this practice.

- Have you experienced God moments that have inspired you to reflect on God during your everyday life? What do you need to do to increase your attentiveness to Godly interruptions?

- Read the passage from Isaiah 40:31 and journal any insights as you ask yourself: *What is God saying to me?*

### Blessing

*May God be with you in the sacredness of real time*
*and into endless time.*
*May your spirit be blessed as you open your heart and mind*
*to the whispers of wonder and awe that surround you this day.*

# CHAPTER 3
## PATHWAY TO INTIMACY WITH GOD

*Wonderings*

*Be still and know that I am God!*
—Psalm 46:10

One day while driving through the backroads of Perry County, Pennsylvania with my windows down, I smelled the fresh mowed hay and heard the bailer tossing the bales out. At that moment, I reconnected with memories of summertime in my childhood when I spent my days making hay, milking the cows twice a day, and all the other barn and field work that needed to be done. This was also the time of my life when I first started my wonderings about God.

As the oldest child, living on a dairy farm meant barn work was my main job. By the time I was about 12 years old, my legs were long enough to reach the tractor pedals. Driving the tractor made the work much more exciting. The summer work was balanced with fun activities such as hayrides, campfires, and softball games, but only after the evening milking was done. Since milking was my least favorite chore, I would occasionally sneak away to a special place in the pasture where I would sit alone by a small stream and, in the stillness, let my thoughts wonder. And, surprisingly, my wonderings were often about God. The wonderings were nothing too introspective, but I remember thinking about God and the great adventure awaiting me (and I was sure that my great adventure would not include milking cows!).

My wonderings were the beginning of my spiritual practice of contemplation. The word *contemplate* means to deliberate, study, and reflect. My habit of retreating to the pasture to be alone and reflect on God became the foundation of my spiritual development. Jesus demonstrated for us the act of finding time to be alone with God in Matthew 14:23b, *"when he went up to the mountain to be by himself and pray."* Designating a time to be alone with God can be quite a challenge, but it is essential for developing your spiritual heart. My time in the pasture became an integral component of establishing a personal connection to God. Oftentimes, children might stare at the clouds and wonder, *Where does God live?* I remember holding grasshoppers in my hand and watching the wind blow through the trees, wondering questions such as, *How did God create our world?* With the eyes of a child, I began to explore more intimate questions: *Where was God in my world?* and *Was I important to God?* Those were the whispers of my heart as I reached out to connect with the Sacred.

> *Rest is not idleness, and to lie sometimes on the grass under trees on a summer's day, listening to the murmur of the water, or watching the clouds float across the sky, is by no means a waste of time.*
> —John Lubbock, 1st Baron Avebury

In exploring the possibility that God knew me and loved me, these wonderings established a connection to the Holy, and the door to my spiritual world opened. It was an adventure that appealed to my child's spirit. These musings were not about discovering the answers to my questions but about developing an attitude of openness of heart and mind to the mysteries of the Sacred. Those moments of wonder ushered me into a lifelong practice of seeking and developing an intuitive awareness of the mystery of the Divine. As I began to recognize God's presence in my life, I delighted in the wonder and awe of those God moments when I felt valued and loved as a child of God. Thus,

I began living out of a contemplative center, a place within my innermost being, my spiritual heart.

As a pediatric chaplain, I was identified by patients, families, and staff as a confidant or a safe person with whom to share their thoughts and feelings. People would oftentimes seek me out or within the context of a visit would share their emotional and spiritual struggles. I brought a sense of the sacred into all conversations and visits. It was not surprising then that as I observed wonderings in the patients, they graciously invited me to enter into a conversation. In order to gain the trust of the children, I began by respecting their space and treating them as valued persons. What I discovered is that children have a secret spiritual life, and if adults take the time to engage a child's trust and listen, we will discover they have *spiritual capacities*.[5] These capacities are profound moments or experiences that influence and shape their inner world as well as provide endurance for living. These spiritual capacities, I believe, allow children to search for relevance or meaning in the midst of their treatment and hospital stay. It is in providing or creating this safe and sacred space that children can be respectfully approached and invited to share. By developing a series of wonder questions, I learned that the children were remarkably open to discussing their wonderings of God. Through these questions, as the children shared their experiences, they introduced me to the sacred and secret discoveries of their world. Professor of psychology Tobin Hart shares significant findings of his research regarding *wonder* as children encounter the spiritual.[6] "Childhood is a time of

---

5 Hart, Tobin. *The Secret Spiritual World of Children: The Breakthrough Discovery that Profoundly Alters Our Conventional View of Children's Mystical Experiences.* Maui, HI: Inner Ocean Publishing, 2003, p. 1.
6 Hart, Tobin. pp. 47–49.

wonder and awe. Children have an inherent openness to mystery, wonder, and delight. What wonder does is help us see the sacred in the world. Wonder keeps the sacred in view and recognizes it alive in our midst." His findings were illustrated throughout this book by his conversations with children as well as interviews with adults as they revealed memories of wonder.

As an activity to engage patients in these wonderings, I used an assortment of small, colored stones. I would offer a handful of stones to a child and ask them to select one that they could keep. Then I would engage them in conversation with introductory questions such as: "I wonder why you selected that color stone?" and "I wonder if this is your favorite color?" Those questions usually provided the opening to something that was a worry or causing them concern. The stones prompted some of my most meaningful conversations.

I once met with a six-year-old in the Pediatric Intensive Care Unit. She was gravely ill for several days and, by the time I was able to visit, she was awake and talking with her mother. When I offered the young girl a choice of colored stones, she said that she chose the blue stone because it was the color of the sky and the sky inspired her to imagine heaven. She shared that earlier in the week, when she was sick, she thought she was going to die and shared her thoughts about heaven. Her mother's surprised face indicated that she hadn't realized her daughter was worried about dying. During the continuing conversation, the girl discussed what she thought about heaven, who would be there to greet her, and how she wondered what dying would feel like. That bedside became a safe and sacred space for this child to reveal her fears and wonderings of heaven. It also provided an opening for her mother to continue to explore these topics.

*Chapter 3: Pathway to Intimacy with God*

One young oncology patient in particular loved the colored stones. In fact, she had her own bag of stones that she had been collecting from all my visits. The twinkle in her eyes and her playful attitude always brightened my day. Whenever we would talk together, her voice would lower to a whisper as she asked me questions that were on her heart. These whispers of her heart revealed her serious contemplation, her wonderings of God's presence in her world. Her story has been an important reminder to me and to those who knew her that children can face painful cancer treatments with amazing courage. The memory of her lively spirit and sweet smile is tucked away in my heart.

Some of my other ways to engage children and teens included coloring in books or mandalas, molding playdough, reading storybooks, and other types of play. These activities were merely an opening to allow the patient to direct the conversation into whatever topic they wanted. One patient and I had our best conversations during numerous games of UNO. Many times, conversations with patients evolved and became sacred moments in which children would reveal their deep thoughts, feelings, anxieties, and fears regarding their illness, treatment, and hospital stay. There were times that a child would share their wonderings or insights about God, including their memories from dreams. Those remarkable visits are cherished treasures that I respect and honor as I do each child. The sacred sharing of the children provided clarifying moments that informed my faith as well as providing a humble reminder that God is present in a child's world.

These conversations with children could only occur when trust was established first, and trust was often built during play. All too often, I have observed adults disregard, talk over, and even ridicule the small voices around them. Gentleness, compassion, and quiet listening inspires trust, inviting children to engage in sharing their deep thoughts. Creating a safe space of acceptance encourages sharing, whether you're a child or an adult. Being overwhelmed with fear of the unknown can be very distressing. Encouraging little ones to express their fears and acknowledging them encourages a healthy attitude and promotes healing. Children are always observing the adults around them. We are teaching them to respect others when we honor and respect them. Opportunities to interact with children are significant treasured moments when we can gift them with words of praise and admiration that affirm their worth rather than showing indifference or even outbursts of harsh words.

> *The first duty of love is to listen.*
> —Paul Tillich, philosopher

Although I have talked mainly about the children who were patients, pediatrics included a range of ages from newborns through 18 years. That meant there were many visits with teenagers, which required a different focus and was more challenging for a variety of reasons. Teens were more aware of their diagnosis and treatment, and were involved in relationships and school activities, which were often disrupted by a hospital stay. Each teen was unique, and I approached each of them as an individual. Initial discussions were commonly focused on the reasons they were there and any topics they considered safe, such as their family, friends, school, and activities. These conversations allowed me to get to know them in a casual manner. Whatever they allowed was enough for that particular time. If their diagnosis or treatment changed at all, it could become a moment of crisis. During that time, I might then be trusted to hear their fears and discuss their feelings about God. In one particular case, a young man about 17 years old was in serious decline after an extensive stay. He requested a visit to discuss a Scripture meditation I had given him during a previous conversation. The meditation focused on Genesis 32 when Jacob wrestled with a man until daybreak. He wanted to discuss the things he wrestled with including his concerns for his mom, since she would be alone after his death. Not all patients were discharged home, so memories of this young man and many others are precious.

**Surrender**

Franciscan friar and spiritual writer Richard Rohr said, "We don't think our way into a new life; we live our way into a new kind of thinking."[7] That must be the starting place for each person as they face a new and deeper way of thinking, believing, and living. It becomes a critical point whereby each person must decide to be vulnerable with God and admit that much of life is out of control. At that time, we must *submit or surrender* our lives as in obedience to Christ's invitation. It is assumed that this type of surrender is done out of a point of weakness and may be considered as giving up. However, I would argue that this is a surrender of strength and it is not *giving up* but instead

---

[7] Rohr, Richard. *Simplicity: The Freedom of Letting Go.* New York: The Crossroad Publishing Company, 2003, p. 58.

*giving over* to God. That's the paradox of the Good News of the Gospels: we must *lose* self in order to *find* self. It is in our surrender that we are liberated to begin our search for newness and fullness of life in Christ.

> *You were taught to put away your former way of life, your old self, corrupt and deluded...and to be renewed in the spirit of your minds.*
> —Ephesians 5:22

## Deck Five

The cruise ship was bound for the Caribbean, and I was escaping the January subzero temperatures in Pennsylvania. We sailed out of Miami and after two days approached our first stop at a small island in the Lesser Antilles. Deck five was my favorite location on our cruise ship. I loved sitting in the morning sun on a lounge chair, reading my devotions and writing in my journal. On this particular morning, I watched as our ship navigated closer to the harbor of our first stop. It was a bright, balmy morning as the sunlight glistened on the water. I was appreciating the different shades of blue sky and turquoise water when a small boat chugged out from the dock and headed straight for our ship. Along the side of this craft were printed the words "Pilot Boat." The boat pulled alongside our much larger vessel, and I watched as the pilot jumped on board our ship. He went directly to the bridge where the captain and his officers were stationed. From my vantage point, I could see the pilot direct and guide the captain through the channel waters of the harbor. As we arrived at the dock, I learned that this was necessary to safely navigate the rocky harbor and avoid damaging the vessel.

This scene reminded me of a sermon illustration I had heard years ago about how when we surrender our lives to Christ, God will be our pilot throughout the dangerous waters of our life. My deck five experience made me realize the accuracy of this comparison. Relinquishing control to God is an essential first step. Change cannot occur until you trust God fully.

## Reflections

- Can you recall a time during your childhood when you engaged in wonderings or thoughts of the Sacred? Journal those insights and memories.

- Consider the concept of surrender or submission and journal your thoughts regarding the following: We must *lose* self in order to *find* self.

- Read Genesis 32 and focus your reflection on verses 24 to 30. Journal these questions: *What do you wrestle with in your life? Where is God in your situation?*

## Blessing

*May the Creator God draw you closer to the Presence by opening your spiritual heart and mind to the childlike wonderings that whisper to your spirit of Divine Love.*

# CHAPTER 4
## PATHWAY TO SPIRITUAL GROWTH

*Silence and Solitude*

> *In the morning, while it was still very dark, he got up and went out to a deserted place, and there he prayed.*
> —Mark 1:35

Silence and solitude are not only prerequisites for creating a sacred space for prayer but are also vital in developing attentiveness to God. Solitude is finding a place to be alone with God where we seek the light in this dark world.[8] It is a place of struggle, conversion, and transformation as we encounter God. In this alone time, God can reveal things to us that we might not want to acknowledge. It is in our vulnerability that we are able to listen with our spiritual ears and accept with our spiritual hearts. It's a time to empty ourselves of the many demands upon us as well as to shed our mantle of roles and responsibilities. In solitude, we are able to discover our true identity in Christ, our true self.

> *The silence is there within us. What we have to do is to enter into it, to become silent, to become the silence. The purpose of meditation and the challenge of meditation is to allow ourselves to become silent enough to allow this interior silence to emerge. Silence is the language of the spirit.*
> —John Main

Silence is a challenge because of the noise, both internal and external, that surrounds us. In silence, we may have a million thoughts clamoring for our attention. Our minds are cluttered and overstimulated by noise. Silence may feel like we're wasting time, and when we sit in silence, we can't really tell if anything is happening. Be assured that God's Spirit is present and at

---

[8] Nouwen, Henri J. M. *The Way of the Heart: Connecting with God Through Prayer, Wisdom, and Silence.* New York: Ballantine Books, 1981, p. 22.

work deep within, beyond our own ability to detect differences within ourselves. God's Spirit is deeper than our thoughts and emotions; transformation is a process. Sometimes silence takes a lot of practice. The longer we practice silence, the more easily we find that the noise slowly recedes and we begin to open ourselves more fully to God. Silence means you must let go of your mental to-do lists, and you must not reflect on fixing your problems. Instead, rest in God's presence. Another approach is to select a word or phrase that will draw you back into God's presence when your mind wanders. For example, the word *peace* may gently remind you that God is awaiting your attention, allowing you to empty your mind and return to rest in God's presence.

During my first silent retreat, it took me almost two days to release the endless chatter that was ongoing in my mind. The retreat leader introduced all the attendees to a practice that helped us to let go of distractions and enter into silence. While sitting in a comfortable position, I would close my eyes and imagine I was sitting by a fast-moving river with the Lord. When a distracting thought came to mind, I would release it into the river and the waters would carry it away. When you are seeking silence in your prayer time, don't give up. Hang in there and keep trying. This practice was able to usher me into the silence and peace I needed to create my sacred space with God. In solitude and silence, we are able to open ourselves to hearing the heart whispers of the Lord.

> *Silence invites us to leave behind the competing demands of our outer world for a time alone with Jesus. Silence offers a way of paying attention to the Spirit of God and what God brings to the surface of our souls.*
> —Adele Ahlberg Calhoun, *Spiritual Disciplines Handbook*

**Devotional Reading**

*Devotional reading* of the Scriptures is my preferred spiritual practice during my time of reflection and being with the Lord. I began this practice of Scripture reading, praying, and journaling my prayers when I was a young mother at home with two little ones. It wasn't until much later in my life that I learned that my own abbreviated practice was a spiritual discipline called *Lectio Divina,* which in Latin means "Divine Reading." Much has been written regarding this ancient Christian practice. The traditional Benedictine practice includes four rhythms or movements that can flow beautifully, one into the other. I often read the Scripture twice or more, silently and aloud, and the text resonates with me differently as I vary my reading style.

As you prepare to engage in this practice, select a time of day when you are most rested and alert. Sit comfortably in your sacred space as you open yourself before God. This is a time of listening and being filled with God's presence. Invite the Lord into this space by saying, "Come, Lord Jesus, Come," or "Here I am, Lord." The movements include the following.

1. Read (*Lectio*): Begin by silently reading the text, slowly and gently as you savor the words and listen with your spiritual heart. You can reread the same passage again, either silently or aloud, listening for a word or phrase that shimmers and catches your attention or speaks to you. Set the text aside, sit quietly, and listen to the phrase that touched you.

2. Reflection or Meditation (*Meditatio*): Linger with the passage and reflect. Allow your memories, hopes, or concerns to interact with the text. Don't allow yourself to be distracted by other thoughts. Journal or jot down words or phrases that speak to your heart. Ask yourself: *What is God saying to me in this text? How does this passage connect to my life at this time?*

3. Respond or Pray (*Oratio*): Enter into an intimate dialogue with God and share your thoughts and feelings. Be authentic. Through the inspired word, allow God to draw you deeper. Draw closer to the Divine and share yourself. Journal your thoughts and your prayer.

4. Rest or Contemplation (*Contemplatio*): In silence, rest and wait in the presence of God. Consider the word(s) you have received. Carry these word(s) with you throughout your day. Delight in the glow of God's love.

We sit in God's presence to listen to God's Word and to allow the Scripture to be absorbed into our spirit. By reading a selected passage, we allow the text and God's Spirit to speak to and inspire us at that particular moment. There is opportunity for growth and trust. Come into God's presence to linger over the Scriptures, not to analyze or intellectualize. This is a spiritual practice to listen with your heart and wait upon God to reveal to you a word of wisdom that invites you "into a deeper way of being with God."[9]

> *Come before the Lord and begin to read. Stop reading when you feel the Lord drawing you inwardly to himself. Now, simply remain in stillness. Stay there for a while.*
> —Jeanne Guyon (1648-1717),
> *Experiencing the Depths of Jesus Christ*

## Teachability

*Teachability*, a spiritual discipline, is demonstrated by being receptive to learning from God through the Holy Spirit's guidance. It is maintaining an open heart, open mind, and open attitude and attentiveness of your spirit throughout your everyday living. Teachability is not confined to educational programs, Bible study, worship, and Scripture reading but is also practiced in a variety of life experiences and interactions with other people.

When I was about 20 years old, I decided to leave my family's church and search for my own faith community. It was in an effort to self-differentiate my faith and values from those of my family. During this time, I discovered a church that reflected my inner yearnings with an emphasis on service. Service was important, since I wanted opportunities to live out my faith in

---

[9] Calhoun, Adele Ahlberg. *Spiritual Disciplines Handbook: Practices That Transform Us*. Downers Grove, IL: InterVarsity Press, 2005, pp. 168–169.

a genuine manner. This church community also introduced me to the ritual of feet-washing, which was the beginning of my appreciation for the richness and beauty of rituals for personal and corporate worship. My quest for a new church community expanded my teachability in many ways, and later in my hospital chaplaincy rituals became touchstones to the Sacred as I cared for a diverse patient population.

It was a few years after getting established in a new church community that I married. My husband and I created a home and had two beautiful daughters. We both felt it was important for my role to be that of a stay-at-home mom because of his long work hours. What I discovered was the plentiful opportunities for learning through volunteering. These opportunities included hosting home Bible studies for moms in the neighborhood, volunteering as a Sunday school teacher and children's director at our church, and leading a Brownie Girl Scout troop. As our children grew older, I served as a youth leader. These many opportunities for service as a volunteer enabled me to develop organizational and leadership skills as well as increased attentiveness to God through my devotional readings. Broadening my creative abilities, I began developing and organizing new programs in Christian education for children and adults. Volunteering was a means of developing my abilities in a way that increased my confidence and allowed me to recognize new opportunities for continued growth.

Teachability is an attitude of eagerness, humility, and openness. Learning new things can happen in a myriad of ways if we are receptive to God's leading.

> *I am about to do a new thing; now it springs forth,
> do you not perceive it?*
> —Isaiah 43:19

**Discernment**

*Discernment* is a spiritual practice that became integrated into my daily devotions as I searched for guidance in my life decisions. I had lots of questions and little knowledge of how to find answers. Within my devotional time, I developed my own unique process that included Scripture reading, prayer, and journaling. By selecting a random passage, I would read and journal my thoughts. In my journal, I would write any words that shimmered or spoke to me and would then ask myself, *What is God saying to me in this text?* What I learned is that discernment is not easy, and you can't hurry the process. Discernment isn't an exact science; it's about further establishing faith and trust in our Lord.

> *Commit your way to the Lord, and trust…*
> —Psalm 37:5

The word *discernment* comes from the Latin word *discernere*, which means "to separate," "to distinguish," "to determine," "to sort out."[10] Henri Nouwen defines discernment as "a spiritual understanding and experiential knowledge of how God is active in daily life that is acquired through disciplined

---

10 Farnham, Suzanne G., et al. Listening Hearts: Discerning Call in Community. Harrisburg, PA: Morehouse Publishing, 1991, p. 23.

spiritual practice. Discernment is faithful living and listening to God's love and direction so that we can fulfill our individual calling and shared mission."[11] To expand on these definitions, there should be an additional emphasis on obedience to maintain the integrity of the process. By continued listening to the still, small voice of God, we are called deeper into the relationship. It is through obedience to God's voice that more discernment follows. Discernment takes place within our intimate relationship with the Lord and our strong commitment to Christ.

Discernment can also happen within a community, whether it is your church community of Bible study, choir, or wherever you share spiritual support. This community can enrich, enable, and affirm your discernment practice. A prerequisite for this type of community is that the people you invite to share your discernment with are trustworthy, can keep confidence, and will hold you accountable as a spiritual friend.

> *Live the questions, perhaps then, someday far in the future, you will gradually, without even noticing it, live your way into the answer.*
> —Rainer Maria Rilke

As I further developed my attentiveness to God, there was a deepening of my faith as I learned more about obedience to God. During those years, I learned about a structured study program for ministry in my denomination. After a lengthy

---

[11] Nouwen, Henri J. M., Christensen, Michael J., Lair, Rebecca J. *Discernment: Reading the Signs of Daily Life*. New York: HarperCollins, 2013, p. 3.

consideration, I entered this program and acknowledged my interest and desire for pursuing a call to ministry. It was an ongoing process that led me to a new pathway. During the late 1980s, there were very few women in this program. In fact, there were only two women licensed to the ministry in my district. I continued praying and searching the Scriptures and journaling my thoughts and, in doing this, realized I had a passion for what was next. The passage from Jeremiah 20:9 illustrates how I felt about a ministry call: *"If I say, 'I will not mention him or speak any more in his name', then within me there is something like a burning fire shut up in my bones; I am weary with holding it in."* This was my confirmation to enter into the study program and to pursue licensed ministry. When I shared this with my husband, he was supportive. We both agreed this did not necessarily mean I would become a pastor, but it was something I could further explore. Later, that would change.

> *Let each of you lead the life that the Lord has assigned, to which God called you.*
> —1 Corinthians 7:17

**Reflections**

- As you focus on the Scripture text from Romans 12:1–3, utilize the movements of Lectio Divina and journal your thoughts, feelings, insights, or images that result from your reflections. What is God saying to you?

- Review your daily routine and notice those places you have opportunities for solitude and silence. Identify and

Sacred Space

let go of any resistance to establishing this practice. Just begin.

- As you review your life, can you identify those times when you were engaged in teachability? What did you learn? Do you maintain this attitude of teachability today?

## **Blessing**

*Hold me in your silence, O Lord, as I delight in your Word.*
*Deepen my desire to discern your will*
*and discover your wisdom within the stillness.*
*May the light of your Word guide me on this journey of life. Amen.*

# CHAPTER 5
## PATHWAY OF STRUGGLE

*Wrong-Way Worship*

> *Worship happens whenever we intentionally cherish God and value God above all else in life. Worship is what is important to us.*
> —Adele Ahlberg, *Spiritual Disciplines Handbook*

When I remember this time of my life, I'm deeply humbled as I recall how God did not abandon me as I struggled to control an unfortunate situation. God had control of the situation, and I had to learn an important lesson: God was to be first in my life. That place of honor does not belong to a spouse, children, or any person or thing; it belongs to God alone. It was a difficult lesson for me as I learned the importance of defining and realigning my priorities for worship.

For most Christians, when they hear the word *worship*, they think of the Sabbath and attending a church service to honor the Lord. During our Sabbath worship, we engage in specific elements such as reading the Gospel, bowing our heads for prayer, and lifting our voices as we sing praise songs. It is a gathering of community as our concerns are shared and offerings are collected. As the sermon is presented, we hear and reflect on stories of Jesus that connect us to our time as we look to our future. Sabbath worship should also include an opportunity for introspection, evaluation, and even correction. It is an appropriate time of accountability as we align ourselves to Godly principles, a time of reflection that could reveal those things we keep hidden even from ourselves. It's in our vulnerability and our examination, if we can be honest with ourselves, that we confront painful and humbling truths.

Worship is also about those things that we place great value on and that give meaning to our lives. Think about those things that give your life significance. What is it that you focus on and plan your life around? Whatever you name as your focus is likely what you worship. Those things we identify as what we love and desire can become an obsession that rules our lives.

Sacred Space

Those things might be money, our work, or power. True worship of our Creator God, though, means that God should maintain the place of honor in our lives. As Calhoun maintains, "True worship does not equal going to church on Sunday. This is not a particularly new thought. Jesus knew people could attend the synagogue while focusing on the closing of their business deal on Monday.... He put it simply, *'These people honor me with their lips, but their hearts are far from me' (Matthew 15:8).* Worship can be offered in the power of the self rather than in response to the Spirit."[12]

> *You shall love the Lord your God with all your heart, and with all your soul, and with all your mind. This is the greatest and first commandment.*
> —Matthew 22:37, 38

In the following illustration, I share about a time in my life when I faced trouble and did not trust in God's leading. Today, I have a different perspective of this situation, because it led to my learning of how struggles may result in spiritual growth. I remain faithful to God and give thanks for these opportunities of transformation.

It was during those years of devoting time and energy caring for my family that I embraced the role of family nurturer. As a busy wife and mom who also worked full time, I was busy filling the role of a typical mom who baked cookies, cooked meals, and cleaned and maintained the home. That's why when

---

[12] Calhoun, Adele Ahlberg. *Spiritual Disciplines Handbook: Practices That Transform Us.* Downers Grove, IL: InterVarsity Press, 2005, p. 45.

my husband told me he had met someone else and was leaving, I was devastated and shocked. My first thought was that these things happen to other families, not ours. My response was one of extreme denial.

As all with all relationships, marriages are complex, and misunderstandings and mistakes are a normal part of what couples deal with. My mistake was assuming that there was something we could do to fix it. It's common for marriages to struggle with a broken relationship and for both partners to decide to dissolve their union. Many people are able to handle it with grace. I did not. By sharing this, I hope to give you a glimpse of how I allowed my feelings to interfere with God's guidance.

In hearing my story, you, I hope, will understand that my husband was a quiet, hardworking man who had a college degree, established his own business, and served as a consultant to many others. He was an outstanding athlete, enjoyed hunting and fishing, and was well-liked. When he started his own business, he devoted many long hours to make it successful. Because of this type of lifestyle, he struggled greatly with his diagnosis of diabetes, which was often out of control. This caused him endless frustration for many years. He also struggled with his own faith questions and became unsupportive of my ministry. These setbacks, as well as other job stresses, contributed to his disappointments in life.

Since I couldn't accept his leaving, I went to numerous counselors, divorce support groups, and even Al-Anon groups. My state of denial continued for several years, and I fervently prayed that God would change this situation. By focusing on problem-solving, I kept asking God to intervene by healing our marriage and relationship. It was soon apparent to everyone around me that I was stuck in the muck and mire of denial. I could not accept the death of our relationship, our marriage, and the loss of a family that I had nurtured for years.

> *Stop trying to protect, to rescue, to judge, to manage the lives around you…remember that the lives of others are not your business. They are their business. They are God's business…even your own life is not your business. It also is God's business. Leave it to God.*
> —Frederick Buechner, *Telling Secrets*

There were several years of the revolving door, moving in and moving out of our home. I felt betrayed, and my anger grew. There were years of arguments about separation and financial issues regarding a divorce settlement. Exhausted, I prayed and watched as the family I had cared for became painfully broken. My denial was so evident that my daughter gave me the album by Aretha Franklin with the song "Respect." Although it is important to have respect for yourself, my focus was on doing whatever I could so that I would have no regrets.

> *You may not control all the events that happen to you, but you can decide not to be reduced by them.*
> —Maya Angelou

Chapter 5: Pathway of Struggle

I realize now that I could not control or stop what was happening to our marriage and to our lives. At the time, I believed that my husband would at some point discover his error. I wanted to give him opportunities to change his mind and return to his family. I was experiencing *regret bias,* which is what happens when people anticipate regret and make choices based on that fear. I knew I would not be able to live with the guilt if I didn't try everything in my power, so I gave ample opportunities to resolve and heal our marriage. Sadly, we were never at the same place at the same time for any resolution.

During this time, my spiritual life was greatly impacted. My prayer time focused solely on my circumstances, my grief, and my disappointment. It was to my detriment that my flawed thinking continued to hinder my intimacy with the Lord. It should have been no surprise when the darkness of doubt and despair descended on my spirit. There were times that I could not pray, and I withdrew into myself. That's when I realized I was at my end, that I could not rely on my previous spiritual beliefs or assumptions to guide me out of the circumstances that overwhelmed me.

This had been a slow process that drained my spiritual vitality and enthusiasm for life. Until I reached my end, I couldn't confront my greatest fear. That's when I realized there was nothing to fear any longer, because my greatest fear had already happened. My family had moved on without me, and I was living alone in our family home. By now, the girls were young adults and living their own lives. We weren't divorced but were living separate lives. That doesn't mean that the love I felt for my husband stopped, and it doesn't mean the care and concern was gone either. But it does mean that I reconciled myself to the fact that I could not control or manage the outcome any longer.

> *Sometimes letting go is an act of far greater power than defending or holding on.*
> —Eckhart Tolle

By neglecting to trust the inner voice of my heart, I didn't allow God's Spirit to guide me. Instead of embracing the fullness of God's grace and love, I had based my response to this situation on my feelings and tried to control others. In this situation, my feelings influenced my spiritual practices, which is a flawed foundation given how inconsistent and unreliable feelings are. There are good reasons to give thanks for those times of darkness, because it was in the dry and barren wilderness that I was able to detach from my *self*, my self-interests and self-will. Before God, I saw and realized my shortcomings. This desert period, the detachment or emptying of self, was an important path to my spiritual humility. By acknowledging my insufficiency, I was able to move into a new understanding with God.

Perhaps that's when I realized I had been embracing the pain instead of embracing the power of God. I had been holding tightly onto pity instead of holding tightly to the promises of the Holy One. When I emptied myself of these woeful attitudes, I was able to be filled with God's blessings of hope. Only then was I able to cross the threshold into Christ's light, which became a beacon out of the darkness of disillusionment. My prayer became, "Thy will be done, O Lord." In submission and obedience, I was drawn to a place of acceptance as well as a sense of renewed understanding and reverence for God. God took me through the struggle, through the confusion, through the sorrow to a deeper self-knowledge. St. John of the Cross calls this deeper self-knowledge "the other knowledge of God," as it proceeds from its source. In the midst of my painful family problems and in spite of my inadequacies, spiritual growth and transformation transpired.

> *Let me know myself, Lord, and I will know you.*
> —St. Augustine

## Reflections

- Was there ever a time when you faced a major struggle in your life? How was it resolved? Journal ways that you experienced God's power and presence.

- Consider the statement below of the four "Ts" and contemplate whether this can be a guide for you in your life's circumstances:

    > When responding to life's *trouble*, recognize the *truth* in the situation and with *trust* in the Lord, give *thanks*.

- Read and reflect on the Scripture text from Isaiah 43:1–4b. As you read, what word(s) from the text speak to your heart? Remember and reflect on those word(s) throughout your day.

## **Blessing**

*May God grant you insight and grace to examine your life.
May Christ's light illuminate those vulnerable places of your heart
and guide you to healing spaces and wholeness.*

# CHAPTER 6
## PATHWAY TO CHAPLAINCY

*Discernment is an Adventure*

> *Let each of you lead the life that the Lord has assigned, to which God called you.*
> —1 Corinthians 7:17

In my obedience to the Lord, I began to focus on my future potential for a new ministry. I began to notice a dissatisfaction with my work and wondered if there wasn't something new and fresh for me to experience in ministry. There was a stirring in my spirit, and I began praying about this in very nonspecific terms. In the beginning, it was only an occasional reflection about other ministry opportunities. I realize now that it was really a matter of God's timing as I began discovering more about this new call to chaplaincy and the Clinical Pastoral Education program.

My discernment had several phases that occurred over a period of one year. I began my search through my daily devotional time using Lectio Divina. I also used journaling as a guide, since I believe the Scriptures are a "living document" that can reveal insights, new understandings, and a new awareness of our circumstances at that moment. I prayed and kept an open mind during conversations throughout my day, listening for a word of wisdom from God. I did not share or discuss with any others my thoughts regarding this discernment process but kept it private until much later. I discovered that God did reveal insights and information through other people. Someone would share an insight from their devotions or a word of encouragement from the Scripture that was meaningful to them and also resonated with me.

My discernment continued as I met a retired hospital chaplain who attended a women's ministry luncheon. She enthusiastically shared stories about the patients she cared for in her hospital ministry and, as she discussed her work, she gave full details about various medical diagnoses and procedures. I had

Sacred Space

doubts that I could ever be involved in hospital ministry, since I often became light-headed and unsteady during hospital visits. I couldn't imagine working in one. Nevertheless, I was inspired by her passion for chaplaincy and for the Clinical Pastoral Education (CPE) program. Her passion motivated me to further investigate the program.

It was a short time later that my uncle was diagnosed with lung cancer. Uncle Paul had smoked since he was 12 years old. My mother called and asked if I would visit him, since he was given only three months to live and wanted to talk. My uncle had always been a gifted storyteller, and our visits were lively and interesting as he shared jokes and many humorous tales from his childhood, some of which I had never heard before. Initially, that's what most of the early visits consisted of. Then our conversations began including discussions about his beliefs, as well as thoughts about life after death. I sat with him and listened with a new awareness of the sacredness of these moments. He had invited me to be a part of his path of preparation for death. It was at time of fear and trembling for us both. I realized how much of a privilege it is to be invited to accompany someone as they prepare for the end of their life. It was with a sense of wonder and reverence that I crossed into this new understanding of creating sacred space. I learned that sacredness can contain more than prayers and Scripture readings. Sacred space also contains stories and jokes, laughter and tears, and sharing of rituals and memories as well as lots of doubts and questions of faith.

Near the end, when he was in hospice care, I received an urgent call to see him. I remember the fear and distress in his eyes. His memory was clouded from the morphine, and he struggled with confusion. He had forgotten the comfort of our conversations. By reading his favorite text, the 23$^{rd}$ Psalm, he joined me in repeating those familiar words and became calmer. By placing his "holding cross" in his hands and praying together, the Lord soothed his spirit. This was one of the last few lucid moments my Uncle Paul had before his death. I recognized what a privilege it was to be a part of his journey. I had crossed a threshold to a new pathway that allowed me to discover the sacredness of end-of-life situations. Paradoxically, I learned that end-of-life can be a time of tension between hope and hopelessness, peace and despair, gladness and sadness.

Having identified chaplain ministry as a calling, I wanted to discover more about CPE and how to become a chaplain. I investigated various CPE programs, completed the online portions of the application, and wrote up the required paperwork, but I had to determine where I should submit these materials. This was an important crossroads, a pivotal point in my life. There were a lot of unknowns if I continued on this path. I struggled with the unfinished business of my marriage and this new call. Did I trust God enough to follow through with this process? My surrender, my time of obedience, had arrived. I gave God the answer as I drove down that steep hill and said, "Yes, Lord, I'll do it." I just didn't know where I was going or how to begin the search.

> *When setting out on a journey, do not seek advice from those who have never left home.*
> —Rumi

It was at that time I read about a spiritual pilgrimage to Albuquerque, New Mexico. The pilgrimage was organized and structured, and all I had to do was attend and listen for God's leading. I went with the primary purpose of discovering a site to apply for CPE. The first group exercise on this pilgrimage was a one-on-one exercise where everyone was paired up with another person. During our time together, we were assigned discussion questions as an activity to get acquainted. My partner was a pastor from central Pennsylvania who was enthusiastic about my interest in CPE and shared some of her experiences. She had a wealth of information regarding program expectations and standards that should guide my decision process. In the midst of our conversation, she emphatically recommended the Rev. Paul Derrickson as an outstanding supervisor of CPE. At that time, he was director of pastoral care at Penn State Hershey Medical Center.

At that moment, I realized I had my answer. The remainder of the pilgrimage helped me to sort through the residual feelings of loss as I planned to leave a ministry I had known and loved for over 14 years. The very night I returned from the pilgrimage, I submitted my application to Penn State Hershey Medical Center for their CPE program. It wasn't long before I was contacted and an interview was arranged. The same week of the interview, I received a call one evening that my husband had a single vehicle accident while out of town. He was flown to Baltimore with head and spinal cord injuries. After surgery for his injuries, he was transferred to a physical therapy center. When he arrived at the therapy center, they did a remarkable job of assisting in recovery and rehabilitation. It was approximately six weeks later on Memorial Day weekend that he was discharged home.

Chapter 6: Pathway to Chaplaincy

During the recuperation and rehabilitation period, I had rescheduled my Hershey interview and was later accepted into the program. The start date for the summer session was the Tuesday immediately following Memorial Day. If I were to begin the program, I would need to move that weekend. After a discussion between the two of us, we couldn't agree on the conditions of my staying. I continued with my plans and left for Hershey.

> *Do what you feel in your heart to be right—for you will be criticized anyway.*
> —Eleanor Roosevelt

## Reflections

- Review your life, and identify moments that you may have felt a "stirring in your spirit." What was the outcome?

- Have you considered that God may be calling you to *something more*? How would you approach learning more about that?

- Utilizing Lectio Divina, focus on the Scripture text: Matthew 14:22–33, or portions of this lengthy passage.

### Blessing

*May the wisdom of God and the freshness of the Holy Spirit*
*guide you to new opportunities for being and doing.*
*May Christ's compassion inspire you to love and*
*enable you to serve in ways beyond your comprehension.*

# CHAPTER 7
# PATHWAY TO CLINICAL PASTORAL EDUCATION
## *New Insights*

> *Discipleship is not limited to what you can comprehend—it must transcend all comprehension. Plunge into the deep waters beyond your own comprehension, and I will help you comprehend even as I do. Bewilderment is the true comprehension. Not to know where you are going is the true knowledge. My comprehension transcends yours. Thus, Abraham went forth from his father and not knowing wither he went. He trusted himself to my knowledge, and cared not for his own and thus he took the right road and came to his journey's end. Behold, that is the way of the cross. You cannot find it yourself, so you must let me lead you as though you were a blind man. Wherefore it is not you, no man, no living creature, but I myself, who instruct you by my word and Spirit in the way you should go. Not the work which you choose, not the suffering you devise, but the road which is clean contrary to all that you choose or contrive or desire—that is the road you must take. To that I call you and in that you must be my disciple.*
> 
> —Martin Luther (Dietrich Bonhoeffer, *The Cost of Discipleship*)

As I began my CPE experience, I felt humbled as I learned more and more about this vitally important ministry. In discovering my preconceived ideologies would be a barrier in my ministry, I was determined to develop an attitude of openness to new understandings if I wanted to develop my skills and abilities as hospital chaplain. It was a time of adventure that altered my life in an important and fundamental way.

As my 15 months of CPE began, I realized there was no going back, no returning to my former life. I resolved to keep my eyes firmly on the goal of completing this rigorous and intense program to the best of my ability. All of my energy was dedicated to my studies as well as clinical assignments and trauma shifts. As part of a five-member group during residency, our education component of the training was one part of our day. The remainder of our day was for patient care in our clinical areas as well as being on-call for traumas and end-of-life events throughout the hospital. Those weeks were terribly exhausting. As much as I needed my rest, there were nights I had difficulty sleeping because of the intensity of the trauma situations. There were some difficult cases that left me with upsetting images, and I had to learn to disassociate myself from them. During this time, I continued my daily devotions, because I considered this preparation for the hospital ministry. This practice enabled me to honor the Lord in everyday encounters with patients, families, and the hospital clinicians. Those precious devotional moments were a reminder to recognize and respect the Holy Presence in a very clinical, sterile environment. The Spirit's guidance and strength assisted in the exhausting and sometimes time-consuming patient and family situations.

In the midst of being with the dying and attending to their families, I learned much about life and living. As I witnessed human suffering, raging grief, and sorrow, I understood how a non-anxious presence could provide support and a sense of calm and comfort in untenable situations. I realized how important it was to be present with people as they struggled with the "why" questions and the doubts of faith. My theodicy of suffering, or my understanding of why God would permit such suffering to happen, was evolving as I learned to *be* with people in their struggles. As they sat with doubts and questions about faith, I struggled with my own. I began to realize that it was in those moments that new understandings are birthed. Our doubts and fears are reconciled into a new assurance that provides hope and peace for a life beyond death. This transformation of faith is a gradual process. It was an awakening for me to realize the richness of this experience. During those long months of CPE, I began to realize this was simultaneously the most difficult and the most fulfilling challenge I had ever faced.

After I concluded my 15-month training, I submitted my resume for several chaplaincy positions. I had some concerns regarding my finances but knew it was all a matter of God's timing for the right position. Finding temporary employment, I was able to stay in my same apartment in the area. After several chaplain interviews in October and a few callback interviews in November, I was concerned about the lengthy hiring process. By December, I was worried and knew that I needed a chaplain position or the hopes of one by the start of January. During Advent, I received a call from a friend in Hershey Medical Center informing me that the pediatric chaplain was leaving and the position was posted.

This became one of those moments you reflect on later in life as a turning point. It was an important time of prayer and discernment as I spent an entire weekend discussing with God my list of reasons why I could not apply for or accept this position. Since I knew the intensity of the pediatric chaplain position and the emotional and spiritual fortitude that would be needed, I resisted. More importantly, I realized that this position would challenge me to go to a much deeper level of faith and trust with the Lord. I wasn't sure I wanted to go to those deep places of doubt where I would wrestle with God as to why children suffer.

My main question for God was: *How can I do this?* After my time of prayer, by the end of the weekend, my question then became: *How can I not?* I submitted my application for the pediatric chaplain position. Three days before Christmas, I was offered the position and started in mid-January.

**Reflections**

- Reflect on your life story and identify times of uncertainty:

  » A time that you may have felt you wanted to give up on your goals. What happened?

  » A time that your courage kept you focused and moving forward. What kept you moving?

  » A time when you were challenged to go to a deeper level of faith and trust with God. What was the outcome?

- Utilize Lectio Divina with the Scripture passage: 1 Kings 19:11–15b.

## Blessing

*May Divine Wisdom inspire you
to continue on your path of discovery.
Embrace with boldness new possibilities
as you release your doubts and fears
to deepen your faith and trust.*

# CHAPTER 8
# PATHWAY TO PEDIATRIC CHAPLAINCY

*Sacred Trust*

> *The place God calls you to is the place where your deep gladness and the world's deep hunger meet.*
> —Frederick Buechner

Acknowledging that there was a sacred trust implied with my response to God's call, I identified the fundamentals of ministry in providing spiritual care for the children, families, and staff of the children's hospital. It was essential to recognize that this was an interfaith environment, which required an attitude of respect and sensitivity for the diversity of faith, culture, race, economics, and lifestyle choices. Information regarding the numerous faith traditions and their important practices was valued and essential. Perhaps even more important was a nonjudgmental and respectful attitude. My interpretation of this attitude as a Christian chaplain meant demonstrating Christ's example of compassionate action. By integrating compassionate action as a witness of Christ's love, I offered kindness, mercy, compassion, and grace in a ministry to vulnerable people overwhelmed with pain and suffering, struggling to make sense out of a senseless diagnosis, accident, or injury. The following quote by Henri Nouwen summarizes my respect for and emphasis on unity within our diversity:

> "The unity of life among us is even deeper and stronger than the diversity between us."[13]

My approach was to identify the similarities of faith, culture, beliefs, and practices as I cared for this community. By recognizing each individual as a human being, as God's creation, the space between us became common ground in which to address the suffering and pain of families. No matter the differences, there was always some common connector that allowed me to be with them in a compassionate, calm manner. Providing a

---

13 Nouwen, Henri J. M., Christensen, Michael J., Lair, Rebecca J. *Discernment: Reading the Signs of Daily Life*. New York: HarperCollins, 2013, p. iii.

non-anxious presence was often uncomfortable as I confronted a wide range of emotions from patients and their families, especially when responding to traumas. The differences between people became less significant when I sat with parents of a child struggling with a potentially life-threatening illness or accident. Painful suffering in those situations is the same regardless of any differences. Oftentimes, demonstrating respect and compassion for others will open an honest dialogue regarding the faith and practices of other traditions.

> *Finding out what particular insights mean to people in other traditions enables us not only to respect but to love the wisdom of other religions.*
> —Thomas Keating

Being in the presence of others as they struggle with their own doubts and questions is uncomfortable but where spiritual growth most often occurs. My own spiritual struggle was to continue reconciling my understanding and assumptions about a loving God to the painful suffering and death of children. By acknowledging my trust in the promise of our Lord Jesus, the promise that is revealed in his suffering, I was able to find a glimpse of meaning in death and resurrection. The deeper I dove into the many questions, I realized I would receive no answers, only more questions. So how could I make sense out of the senseless suffering that I was witnessing? Somehow, God led me to reconcile my ministry to a place of understanding that, although I could not stop suffering, I could alleviate the suffering by accompanying others in their painful struggle, by gently reminding them of God's love and presence in their difficulties and by embodying an attitude of reverence for God. As I continued in this ministry, new understandings were slowly evolving and revealed to me through the lens of faithfulness and trust in God. Through every encounter with patients and their families as well as the staff and my peers, this foundation of faith permeated my spirit and was reflected in my spiritual care, especially for end-of-life situations. With my spiritual heart, I approached end-of-life with attentiveness for the Presence at the bedside. This ministry was a crossroads to a new aspect of my spiritual life and continued to mold and shape my faith into something more fluid and sustaining.

The end-of-life sacred space was created to invite the presence of the Divine, and by respecting the dying and their family and honoring their faith, beliefs, and traditions. This important space was designed to: recognize the love for the patient by the family members with rituals that might include rubbing sweet-smelling oil on the patient, sharing stories of their memories, reading the patients' or families' favorite poems or Scriptures, singing the patients' favorite songs, and surrounding the patient with their favorite stuffed animals or photos. These and other end-of-life rituals are important, because they create a comforting memory for the family and friends of the patient as they enter into the grief process.

## St. Benedict's Rule

As I wanted to provide the best possible care to those I served, I continually reviewed how I could improve upon my practices. While reading through the various parts of St. Benedict's Rule, I realized there were aspects within it that were reflected in the main objectives of my ministry. St. Benedict lived during the fourth and fifth centuries, prior to the Reformation. The Rule was intentionally written for men and women in the Benedictine communities. Yet today, the Rule is considered one of the great religious classics, inspiring many people. Elements of the Rule that I recognized in my evolving ministry are presented to you in a simplistic manner; the Rule is more extensive in its entirety. Each part or movement is interconnected, and as they flow together, they are interwoven by common themes. The three parts of the Rule I will emphasize will not necessarily be presented in the same order of St. Benedict's Prologue.[14] To preface, it's important to emphasize the omnipresence of God. That is, God is always fully present and involved in all of our everyday lives. God is not in a faraway place, but within and as close to us as our next breath.

> *When you talk, you are only repeating what you already know. But if you listen, you may learn something new.*
> —Dalai Lama

The first word in the Prologue of St. Benedict's Rule is *listen*. The type of listening done with the spiritual heart is listening done through the true innermost self, not the head. It means to listen with sensitivity and compassion, and to listen not only with the hospitality of welcome of an open door but also with the open heart and the open mind.[15]

---

14 Clarke, Lowther W. K., A Pax Book. London: SPCK Publishing, 1931. http://www.solesmes.com/sites/default/files/upload/pdf/rule_of_st_benedict.pdf

15 de Waal, Esther. Seeking God: The Way of St. Benedict. Collegeville, MN: Liturgical Press, 1984.

Listening to God has already been established as essential in our spiritual growth. Always listening, I have been diverted from my original plan for the day many times. In moments of hearing from a nurse about a difficult case, being notified from my pager of a trauma situation, or learning about an end-of-life situation from a clinician, I listened and allowed those moments to guide me. Sometimes, an elevator meeting with an emotional parent diverted me to the cafeteria where, over a cup of coffee, an exhausted and overwhelmed mother of a patient would share her struggles. Elevator moments were God moments when God would intersect with my planned activities and redirect me to those places of need. As it tells us in Isaiah 41:1, *"Listen to me in silence....let the people approach, let them speak."*

By carefully listening, we may hear the pain of the person sharing a new diagnosis, hear the sorrow of the parent whose child died in an accident, or hear the suffering of a new parent learning of their baby's incurable disease. Listen and hear the words with your head, and as you allow the words to resonate, let them speak to your heart.

Flowing from listening and hearing, we can move into *obedience* as an important part of St. Benedict's Rule. As I listen to and hear God's leading, it's of utmost importance to obey by responding. By seeking God's guidance in our lives, a response is required. Be aware that no response is indeed a response. Obedience requires action to what we have heard. Obedience can be difficult on occasion; it is not for the fainthearted and requires courage. One time, I was called to a trauma case, because they needed me to confront and calm an angry young man, the parent of a child who had suffered critical injuries.

Security knew that if this man acted out in his anger, they would be required to restrict him from entering the hospital and from being with his child. The patient's dad was visibly upset as he was pacing outside the emergency room doors, awaiting the arrival of the ambulance. As I spoke with and listened to this very tall, muscular, and furious dad, I did so with kindness and respect. There followed several hours of caring for him by giving him information about the procedures and keeping him updated about his child's progress. His anger gradually diffused as I arranged a consult with the trauma physician, accompanied him to see his daughter in a trauma room, and then escorted him to her room after she was admitted. After several hours, he came to me and apologized for his attitude and belligerence. He explained that he blamed himself for the accident, and his anger was directed at himself and not anyone else. He expressed his gratitude for my willingness to be with him throughout the process. Sometimes, obedience requires us to suspend judgment and to be respectful in situations that are uncomfortable or may appear risky. If we assess a situation too quickly when we don't have all the facts, we may miss an opportunity to share God's love and peace with someone in need.

> *No, the word is very near to you; it is in your mouth and in your heart for you to observe.*
> —Deuteronomy 30:14

St. Benedict's Rule also focuses on *stability or steadfastness* to the faith, to our call, to our response and obedience to Christ throughout our life. To stand firmly in our faith, we are required to be grounded by the Scriptures that guide and support our life. Within that stability, our faith is based on the foundation of obedience, our response to Christ's call, and claim on our lives is contained. As it says in Matthew 7:26, *"And everyone who hears these words of mine and does not act on them will be like a foolish man who built his house on sand."*

Persevering in our faith, we remain firm as we face obstacles, opposition, and cynics who try to undermine our beliefs and principles. Even remaining steadfast to your calling can be a challenge. There were times I questioned: *What am I doing here in this hospital? What do I have to offer these people who are suffering?* I would then reexamine the Scriptures that supported my call, review the places in my life where I saw God's guidance, and then humbly ask God to guide me to the next patient, family, or staff member who had a need. It's important to remember your call.

Standing firmly in our faith, we venture into places of uncomfortable silence, and we confront the angry and confused as they deal with staggering grief and overwhelming situations. Remaining strong in our faith, we cry with those suffering sorrow and loss. As it says in Matthew 7:24, *"Everyone then who hears these words of mine and acts on them will be like a wise man who built his house on rock. The rain fell, the floods came, and the winds blew and beat on that house, but it did not fall, because it had been founded on rock."*

Consistent daily devotions grounded my ministry and enabled me to return to the hospital every day. Embracing spiritual humility, my listening and stillness enabled me to be present in transformative holy moments of sharing of powerful stories, struggles, sorrows, and faith.

**Reflections**

- Do you agree or disagree with Henri Nouwen's quote: *The unity of life among us is even deeper and stronger than the diversity between us.* Reflect on your opinions of diversity among faith traditions, culture, race, and lifestyles. Journal your thoughts.

- Review listening, obedience, and steadfastness. Which of these three would you like to focus on to strengthen your spiritual life? Journal your response.

- Using Lectio Divina to guide you, reflect on and journal the passage from Matthew 7:24–27.

**Blessing**

*May God open your heart and mind to listen for Divine wisdom, reassure you in your obedience as you respond courageously, and encourage you to remain firmly grounded in your faith.*
*Amen.*

# CHAPTER 9
## PATHWAY OF SORROW

*Suicide Loss*

> *Likewise the Spirit helps us in our weakness; for we do not know how to pray as we ought, but that very Spirit intercedes with sighs too deep for words. And God, who searches the heart, knows what is the mind of the Spirit, because the Spirit intercedes for the saints according to the will of God.*
> —Romans 8:26-27

It was the first week in August, and I had spent several sleepless nights with a nagging uneasiness. It was an unsettled feeling that I attributed to the ongoing, strained relationship with my husband. We were meeting together at the end of the week to further discuss divorce. It was the sense of apprehension that finally prompted me to go to the home of Christian friends for insight. Still, the restlessness continued. That Wednesday morning, after visiting patients on the oncology unit, I walked to my office to begin documenting my chart notes. While there, my office phone rang, and on the other end of line was my daughter's voice. She told me that Russ had attempted suicide and was in surgery. I had barely hung up the phone when I received more calls from family members confirming the tragedy and asking how they could help. My colleagues and friends from Pastoral Services surrounded my desk with hugs, prayers, kindness, and support. My brother drove to Hershey to pick me up so that I wouldn't have to drive alone. When we arrived at the hospital, the surgery was completed, and Russ was admitted to the ICU. It was a time of emotional turmoil where we were all overwhelmed with pain and disbelief. He died the following evening.

There are not sufficient words to describe the shock, pain, and horror I felt when I heard this news. The grief and sorrow of this tragedy was as complex as it was interminable. Mental health professionals and counselors refer to this type of grief as *complicated grief,* because grievers are actually dealing with trauma as well as grief.[16] There are many emotions common to

---

16 Survivors of Suicide Loss Task Force. "Responding to Grief, Trauma, and Distress After a Suicide: U.S. National Guidelines." National Action Alliance for Suicide Prevention. April 2015. https://www.sprc.org/sites/default/files/migrate/library/RespondingAfterSuicideNationalGuidelines.pdf.

suicide loss survivors, which may include anguish, shame, guilt, blame, anger, numbness, shock, and denial. Complicated grief is prolonged and may cause so much distress that it interferes with functioning. Healing from suicide loss cases takes many years as the bereaved struggle in the attempt to make sense of the death of their loved one. Suicide loss survivors can be overwhelmed with questions of guilt and blame for not being able to recognize the signs as well as not being able to prevent the tragedy. Survivors can also get caught in the "if only" framework of thinking or self-blame thinking when, in reality, there were underlying, complex mental health issues at work. Attempting to assign blame to someone for a death by suicide is uncalled for and unjustified. Assuming the blame for someone's death by suicide is actually pretentious or grandiose. The decision and the suicide act itself belongs to that individual. It is solely their responsibility and a part of their life story, and it is not anyone else's place to take that away from them.

Suicide is traumatic. "Death by traumatic means isn't uncommon including homicide, accidental injury, medical emergency, war, terrorism, and natural disaster. Suicide, the process of taking one's life in this way can be construed as an act of violence against the self. When the death of a loved one involves trauma, there is a chance that whatever violence occurred, the deceased will traumatize the bereaved."[17] Those who have lost a loved one to suicide often feel at fault. They ask questions such as: *Why didn't I see this? Why wasn't I able to prevent it?* Many suicide loss survivors struggle for years with the unanswerable

---

[17] Survivors of Suicide Loss Task Force. "Responding to Grief, Trauma, and Distress After a Suicide: U.S. National Guidelines." National Action Alliance for Suicide Prevention. April 2015. p. 15. https://www.sprc.org/sites/default/files/migrate/library/RespondingAfterSuicideNationalGuidelines.pdf.

questions that linger. Unfortunately, it's difficult for survivors to think back on happy memories or share stories. Instead, survivors agonize over the past as they question: *Was he really happy? Were they really good years that we had?* In some cases, suicide loss survivors turn to self-destructive responses. Some turn to alcohol or drug use to numb the pain. Others may try to reenact their loved one's steps, indicating that survivors are also at high risk of a suicide attempt. Oftentimes, the bereaved suffer from post-traumatic stress disorder. All of these possibilities reinforce how extremely important it is that suicide loss survivors receive the necessary grief support.

Undoubtedly, there were many times I blamed myself for this tragedy. Even though we were separated and living apart for several years, I felt the shame of suicide. I may have been projecting, but it also felt as though I was being blamed by others. In either case, it felt as if I had a sign around my neck that read, "My husband committed suicide." I couldn't give up and hide by staying in my house. I had to get up every day, pull myself together, and continue living by going to work. In order to do that, I had to *give it over.* Give it over to God and pray for strength to cope each moment, each hour, each day. Give it over and set aside the pain, so I could be with others in their pain.

There are moments of intense suffering and sorrow during grief. I experienced a physical pain and heartache that would devastate me. On one particular day, my pain and sorrow were so intense that I became physically ill. It was during this meltdown that a wonderful sense of peace enveloped me. As my tears stopped, the pain was gone and in its place was a peace that I have never felt before. God pulled me back from the brink of despair and provided the comfort I needed at that time.

Grief is hard work. It's one of the most painful experiences an individual ever faces regardless of the cause of death. Feelings of shock, anguish, anger, regret, fear, anxiety, loneliness, unhappiness, depression, and feeling overwhelmed are integral. With suicide, the bereaved are also overwhelmed by shame and the stigma of suicide. Because of this stigma, many keep the cause of death of their loved one a secret. The need for secrecy prevents the suicide loss survivors from receiving the grief support needed as they deal with the guilt and blame associated with their loss. By suppressing the truth, the stigma of suicide is perpetuated, and this unhealthy cycle continues. Secrecy also circumvents an important part of the grief process in which the bereaved share stories about important memories of their loved one.

There are important elements of compassionate grief care that will assist in the suicide loss survivors in their healing process, helpful words and attitudes that will ease them in their pain. First, recognize that this is a tragic loss; any sudden death is devastating. Acknowledge the death and express your sorrow to the bereaved. Suicide loss survivors should be treated with kindness and compassion as with any other bereaved. Use the name of their loved one in expressing your sympathy, and share your concern for them. Second, don't avoid the bereaved during this tragedy even if you are uncomfortable. Just show up! Even if you don't know what to say, be present and show genuine interest and concern.

> *The word LISTEN contains the same letters as SILENT.*
> —Alfred Brendel

Third, encourage openness by being accepting of the survivor's feelings of sadness, anger, or silence, and providing a listening presence. Just LISTEN. Do not offer your opinions or stories of other cases of suicide or other losses. Recognize that many quotes are not appropriate at this time and can increase distress. One of the worst things said to me was, "God doesn't give us more than we can handle!" When overwhelmed with grief, this statement did not offer comfort, because I didn't feel like I could handle it. A genuine way to show compassion would be to simply say: "I can't imagine how you feel, but I want you to know I care." When in doubt, simply show your support by being present.

Fourth, be patient and encourage the bereaved to share stories of their loved one. Allow them to repeat them, because these stories are very comforting. In fact, it's an important part of healing in the grief process. Listening to these stories is an important role of the community in providing compassionate grief care. Stories of their loved one represents a life lived, and under the stigma of shame and blame, families cannot freely share their memories. Important stories are set aside, which is disruptive to the grief process. It then appears as if their loved one's final act sums up their life. These are important stories and memories that must be shared as a legacy of love.

> *Let everyone be quick to listen, slow to speak, and slow to anger....*
> —James 1:19

## The Stigma of Suicide

The stigmas surrounding mental health as well as suicide in our society contribute to the isolation and lack of support for persons struggling with depression and mental illnesses as well as other at-risk factors that contribute to the spiral of suicide. It's important to note that other at-risk factors can be attributed to post-traumatic stress disorder, which many times include military personnel, police officers, and first responders. In an article from *Psychology Today*, Dr. Deborah Serani explains that "suicide is a death like no other. Based on the accounts of those who have attempted suicide and lived to tell about it, we know that the primary goal of suicide is not to end life, but to end pain."[18] As we continue as a society to make some sense of this, we need to recognize the significant impact of depression. Serani highlights this by describing how "depression narrows their problem-solving skills and this corrosive thinking reduces optimism, the hope of possibility and increases feelings of helplessness." Mental illness seriously limits the choices of the individual.

Statistics shared at a recent Suicide Prevention Conference indicated that one of the demographics with the highest rates of suicide loss is white males in their middle years ages 35 to 64.[19] The main triggers or contributing factors for potential suicide include: untreated and undiagnosed depression (the number one cause in approximately two-thirds of men's suicides); loss of economic productivity; alcohol or substance use; illness, disability, or chronic medical conditions including a new diagnosis of severe

---

18 Serani, Deborah. "Understanding Survivors of Suicide Loss—Suicide is a Death Like No Other." Psychology Today, Nov. 25, 2013. www.psychologytoday.com/us/blog/two-takes-depression/201311/understanding-survivors-suicide-loss.
19 Suicide Prevention Resource Center. "About Suicide."2016. www.sprc.org/about-suicide.

illness; financial stress, both ongoing and immediate (loss of job); criminal justice issues; and intimate partner issues such as divorce, separation, and custody issues. The overall suicide rate has grown by nearly 30 percent over the past 15 years in every demographic category.[20] Every 12 minutes, there is a suicide in the United States. For every death, 146 people are touched, including not only family but also coworkers, emergency response teams, and medical personnel. This means that hundreds of thousands of people grieve through this tragic loss every year.[21]

> *Our lives begin to end the day we become silent about things that matter.*
> —Martin Luther King Jr.

**Faith Communities and Suicide**

Recognizing the many people whose lives are impacted by suicide every year and the complicated grief that accompanies such an act, important questions are raised regarding the role of our religious communities in these people's lives. There is a noticeable lack of information regarding mental illness and suicide on the part of some Christian faith communities. While some denominations have prepared statements and resources for their pastors and congregations, others have neglected to recognize the widespread increase in suicide and the large number of people affected by it, and have failed to do more in addressing these concerns.

---

20 National Institute of Mental Health. "Suicide." May 2018. www.nimh.nih.gov/health/statistics/suicide.shtml.
21 Suicide Prevention Resource Center. "About Suicide." 2016. www.sprc.org/about-suicide.

One of the biggest challenges is the mindset of the faith communities that all suicide is a sin. Under the guise of that blanket statement, faith communities do not consider that mental illness is a primary factor in suicide. This lack of information and understanding contributes to the stigma and shame of suicide. As a result, suicide loss survivors suffer additional pain; as their loved one is condemned by the faith communities, there is no one to support them in their grief. Consequently, many bereaved are not comfortable sharing their feelings with an uninformed community because of these judgmental opinions and are further isolated. In addition, oftentimes uninformed faith communities are not aware of how to provide grief care for the complicated grief that the bereaved struggle with. The responsibility lies heavily on leadership to encourage openness and dialogue within their communities. To enable this dialogue, leadership can:

- educate pastors and congregations regarding the importance of mental health and suicide prevention with the community resources already in place,

- utilize these resources by planning open forums for individuals, families, schools, and other community groups and inviting mental health and suicide prevention groups to discuss identifiable at-risk behaviors,

- and teach nonjudgmental approaches to providing mental health resources and convey the importance of complex grief care to suicide loss survivors.

Resourcing our faith communities on these issues will be preventative measures that could break through the barriers of the stigma of suicide and open the door for education, understanding, and compassionate grief care. This is an important first step. At the heart of suicide is silent suffering, for those with depression and mental illness as well as those struggling in their grief process. With increased awareness, knowledge, and understanding, we are empowered to change lives and enabled to provide compassionate care for healing. The continued alienation and isolation places suicide loss survivors at further risk. The pathway through grief begins with acknowledgement and understanding, and requires support from counseling, support groups, therapy, and faith communities. The theologian Lewis Smedes wrote that "the church must do more than teach about suicide, for the church's primary task is to be the people of God. A church must hear the stories of pain, suffering, and failure in the lives of its members; those who tell the stories must receive from the church both lamentation and the healing balm of Christ. When the church is open and honest about pain and suffering, it can then confront in love even the most difficult of human crises and failures—suicide."[22]

Christian communities are established upon the foundation of the suffering of Christ, the sacrifice of his life upon the cross. When we begin addressing the reality of mental illness and suicide within our faith communities, we acknowledge that this should be a safe place that supports and encourages those who suffer to share the truth of their stories and their pain. The label of "unpardonable sin" becomes another barrier to hope and healing. Indeed, this label further isolates those grieving as they struggle with feelings of shame and guilt that persist under the stigma of suicide. There are several instances of suicide depicted within Scripture, including the account of King Saul (1 Samuel 31:2–5). My assertion is that it is not regarded as unforgivable in these accounts. My reflection upon Romans 8 enables me to see

---

22 Smedes, Lewis. "Is Suicide Unforgivable?" Christianity Today, July 10, 2000. www.christianitytoday.com/ct/2000/July10/30.61.html.

the hope and promise of God's love through Jesus Christ. All of life is valued as a sacred gift, and self-destruction should not be condoned or encouraged. However, spiritual leaders and pastors can promote a spiritual perspective that balances our faith along with an understanding of mental illness that will give a sense of hope to the bereaved.

> *For I am convinced that neither death, nor life, angels, nor rulers, nor things present, nor things to come, nor powers, no height, nor depth, nor anything else in all creation, will be able to separate us from the love of God in Christ Jesus our Lord.*
> —Romans 8:38–39

During the spring of 2008, an Interfaith Suicide Prevention Dialogue was held in Rockville, Maryland. At that gathering, faith leaders represented a variety of traditions, including Buddhist, Christian, Hindu, Jewish, and Muslim communities and together developed a Consensus Statement from their dialogue. A portion of that statement follows:

> Life is a sacred gift, and suicide is a desperate act by one who views life as intolerable. Such self-destruction is never condoned, but faith communities increasingly support, rather than condemn, the *person* who contemplates or engages in suicidal behavior. They acknowledge that mental and substance use disorders, along with myriad life stressors, contribute significantly to the risk of suicide. And they reach out compassionately to the person who attempts suicide and to families and friends who have

been touched by a suicide or suicide attempt. This increasingly charitable understanding finds agreement between the historic precepts of faith and a contemporary understanding of illness and health. It renders no longer appropriate the practice of harshly judging those who have attempted or died by suicide.[23]

> *Based on the accounts of those who have attempted suicide and lived to tell about it, we know that the primary goal of suicide is not to end life, but to end pain.*
> —Deborah Serani, Psy.D.

As a people of God, our communities should be offering suicide loss survivors acceptance, compassion, and support as they accompany them in their grief. Instead of focusing on judgement and condemnation, there should be an emphasis of assurance that God was present in those last moments. The all-knowing God of our past, present, and future understands and knows our painful struggles throughout the whole of our life's story. In those final moments, God does not abandon us in our need. Even as those we love struggle to end their life, in their struggle, God was present. Knowing God was present at the end is a comfort to me. There is no need to offer judgement; God alone is our judge. Whether it's an individual with cancer struggling with pain at the end of their life or an individual with mental illness struggling with pain at the end in their suicide, God

---

[23] Suicide Prevention Resource Center. "The Role of Faith Communities in Preventing Suicide: A Report of an Interfaith Suicide Prevention Dialogue." Newton, MA: Education Development Center, Inc., 2009. http://www.sprc.org/sites/default/files/migrate/library/faith_dialogue.pdf.

does not abandon nor allow us to struggle alone. As individuals, our judgment is God's business.

My chaplain ministry in the children's hospital has demonstrated repeatedly that the times of birth and death are sacred. God is present in those sacred moments and provides indicators of Presence. It is through our awareness and attentiveness to the whispers of the spiritual heart that we are uniquely blessed to be included in these experiences. In birth as in death, we are not alone. The Divine is as close as our own heartbeat.

> *Remember that the lives of others are not your business. They are their business. They are God's business...even your own life is not your business. It also is God's business. Leave it to God.*
> —Frederick Buechner, *Telling Secrets*

**Children and Suicide**

Based on the Pennsylvania Child Death Review Annual Report compiled in 2016, suicide is a continued threat to our children and teens.[24] According to the National Institute of Mental Health's 2016 Suicide Statistics, there were 436 deaths by suicide of children ages 10 to 14 years nationwide. As a pediatric chaplain, I was involved in caring for the parents, family, and friends of children who died by suicide. It's very difficult to accompany parents into a trauma room to see their

---

24 National Institute of Mental Health. "Suicide." May 2018. www.nimh.nih.gov/health/statistics/suicide.shtml.

child after they have attempted suicide and the medical team has unsuccessfully resuscitated the child. The helplessness and hopelessness of a parent at such a time is inconceivable. When there are no words to take away the painful reality of a senseless death, ministry of presence is offered by coming alongside a parent at the bedside, holding their hand, getting them to sit down and rest when weary, and attending to their various needs. Words are not really needed or important unless the family requests prayer or Scripture. It is the compassionate action—the care, calmness, kindness, and gentleness in the chaplain's presence—that assists in the initial grieving process.

In the majority of children and teen suicide cases I was involved in, most were attributed to bullying along with isolation from friends and family. Strong community support, that interconnectedness we all rely on for healthy relationships, is vitally important for children as well as adults. Statistics indicate that there is an alarming increase in suicides. The Suicide Awareness and Prevention programs across our nation have resources, such as education programs for schools and communities, that identify at-risk behaviors in the prevention of suicide, as well as grief resources. There is an increased need for parents, schools, and communities to advocate for information, support, and counseling. This is a nationwide problem that won't be resolved quickly. In our faith communities, Christian education programs and resources for children and youth need to offer more information on mental illness and suicide prevention. Faith communities oftentimes have opportunities within their programs to provide education and awareness of at-risk behaviors through their supervision of participants and through the relationships that are established. Faith communities have a unique role in being able to assist greatly in suicide prevention.

## Legacy

Legacy for those loved and lost to suicide is important, because their life should not be defined by their last act. Suicide loss survivors can reframe their loved one's life by creating a legacy that is life-affirming, a legacy that can be honored and shared by family and passed on. Generally, a legacy is thought of in terms of the tangible with material value, such as property and money, but intangibles can be of unique and greater value. This value is not based on monetary worth but is rather based on memories and stories that we tuck away in our heart. This type of legacy is often the most cherished and is embraced with fondness and love. There is powerful healing and meaning held within this type of legacy that is incomparable and highly valued.

Elisabeth Kubler-Ross wrote, "most people on their deathbed want to know only three things: Have I given and received love? Did I live my life or someone else's? Have I left the world a little better than I found it?"[25] By asking these questions and using them as a guide, we are able to focus on the things to include in our loved one's legacy. You might include: (1) loving stories and fond memories, including photos and memorabilia, (2) impact of their professional career, friends, sports, and other activities, and (3) influence on family and friends. This is only a place to begin; you may have even more ideas that would contribute to the value and other aspects of your loved one's life.

By reframing your loved one's life, you are creating a legacy that honors them. It becomes a legacy of hope and love that is life-affirming and not based on their final act, a legacy that

---

25 Newhouse, Meg. "Legacy: A Powerful Rite of Passage." *Social Network Today* 10, no. 3 (May/June 2010): 6.

can be cherished by the surviving family and friends, and that will influence their lives in a positive and healthy manner. One family shared that their legacy was a scrapbook they created, filled with pictures, news clippings, and mementos of their loved one. Each child in the family owned a copy of this scrapbook. Other families have made quilts that were illustrated with pictures and other items that represented their loved one. There are many more stories and ideas, so allow yourself to be inspired to create your own special legacy that is affirming of life and love and can be passed on.

**Shadow of Sorrow and Refuge**

After returning to work, I struggled with the overwhelming weight of sorrow, a shadow that lingered with me for a timeless period. I remember when I first realized there really seemed to be a shadow with me. It was early evening on a work day; I had stayed long after my quitting time. I was walking inside the parking garage when I looked down on the cement and saw my shadow. Yet, there appeared to be a second shadow also walking alongside me. In order to find some valid reason for this additional shadow, I surveyed the various light fixtures and their angles. After observing this for several days, I realized I didn't want a logical explanation for the shadow. I had already accepted that the shadow was God's Presence, a presence of peace that I felt throughout my day. This presence seemed to lighten the shadow of sorrow that was a very heavy load.

In the book of Psalms, a verse reminded me of God's comfort: *"All people may take refuge in the shadow of your wings."* (36:7) With the shadow as a reminder of God's presence, I didn't feel alone any longer. The shadow of sorrow that weighed me

## Sacred Space

down now became a shadow of refuge. This was an important realization, because suicide loss survivors often feel very isolated. Isolation can lead to a mindset that the stigma of suicide means you are unworthy and undeserving of forgiveness, healing, and love. The shadow of refuge represented acceptance and love that allowed me, through grace, to work through those feelings. Grief is a process, and everyone has a different pace for sorting through complex feelings. The important thing to remember is that you will get through this.

During my grief, I oftentimes had dreams that caused me despair. Whenever I could, I would record a dream in my journal and pray about it. Sometime later, I read that our memories are interwoven so deeply with the person we have loved and lost that dreams and visions are a way of coping with our loss. These dreams may be of comfort, a gentle reminder of the love you have shared with another. Many people have talked with me about feeling the presence of their loved one and speaking to them. Remember to be gentle with yourself during these times.

> *Hope is the thing with feathers*
> *That perches in the soul*
> *And sings the tune without the words*
> *And never stops at all.*
> —Emily Dickinson

There was a period of time when I kept losing my car. These occurrences happened most often at work where I parked in the designated employee levels of the hospital parking garage.

*Chapter 9: Pathway of Sorrow*

Yet whenever I left work at the end of my day, I couldn't find my car. I'd start on one level, walking through with my key remote, pressing the unlock button and hoping I was close enough to hear the horn. It became such a problem that I kept post-it notes in my car to write down the level and location in the garage. Eventually, this became a joke to my coworkers, which was further solidified at our department Christmas party. I had parked on a side street near the restaurant, and as we were leaving after dinner, some friends laughed about whether I could find my car. Not realizing that it had snowed, I assured them I would find it. After walking for several minutes through several snow-covered streets and looking at the snow-covered cars, I realized that I had lost my car, again. A few moments later, my friends drove up and stopped to check on me, knowing that I probably would not be able to find my car. They not only helped me, but they also understood me. Identify those friends you have who are kind, understanding, and provide support.

There were also instances when I worried about the blank spaces in my memories of the suicide and afterward. It seemed as though I couldn't remember things, and that was worrisome as it continued for quite a while. As I struggled with the realities of the suicide, a blanket of numbness covered my mind and some memories or thoughts were just lost. One day, this became evident in a conversation with my daughter. We were discussing something that happened after her dad's death, and I realized that I had no recollection of it at all. In her wisdom, she said to me, "Mom, maybe you don't remember and that's okay. Maybe you don't need to remember." Learn to be patient with yourself.

Patience was what I needed when I realized that I couldn't focus to read or even to pray. In the midst of mind-numbing grief, I couldn't concentrate. One sentence of Scripture would be all I could focus on, and my prayers would consist of only one or two words. I knew others were praying for me and that was a comfort. Be patient and understand that this will change.

**Reflections**

- Are you aware of the Mental Health and Suicide Prevention resources available in your community? Thoughtfully consider the ways you can obtain and share those resources with others in your faith community.

- Consider a time when you struggled with feelings of isolation from others. As you remember those feelings, meditate on the following words, repeating them often as you absorb them into your mind and heart.

*Peace be still and know,*
*I am precious and honored,*
*I am loved by God.*

- Reflect on the Scripture text from Ecclesiastes 3:1–8, and journal your thoughts.

**Blessing**

*May the Divine Spirit*
*open your mind, open your heart*
*to the suffering of others.*
*Open your hands and offer your prayers.*
*Abide in Christ's love.*

# CHAPTER 10
## PATHWAY TO HEALING

*Gentle Healing*

> *Forgive and you will be forgiven.*
> —Luke 6:37

Shortly after Russ's suicide, I returned to my pediatric chaplain's position and determined that I would do whatever necessary to keep my own grief from interfering with my ministry. It was a struggle for me to accept what I had told others in my ministry: "Be gentle with yourself." Grieving is hard work. Don't expect to do this work swiftly, and don't give yourself a deadline or limit on how long you will grieve. I was surprised that small triggers could throw me into a vortex of grief that sucked the life out of me. It didn't matter where I was or what I was doing; if a memory was suddenly triggered, I became emotional. I understand now that this is normal and very common in grief. How we respond to these emotional reactions is something we have to determine for ourselves. Generally, when this happened, I would give myself permission not to do anything too emotionally demanding. That means, if working, I would spend more time doing administrative work. When not at work, I would not expend too much energy because I was already drained. Everyone has to consider their circumstances and do what's best. Embrace an attitude of gentleness and patience with yourself.

**Embrace Grace**

As believers in Christ, we recognize that God's grace, though unmerited, is offered freely. An important attribute of our spiritual life is to extend forgiveness, to ourselves and to others. The first type of forgiveness, often one of the hardest, is forgiveness of self. This is not about anyone else; it is only about you and your own quality of life. To move into healing and wholeness, it's necessary to let go of the wounds you carry. Forgive yourself for all those things that have accumulated in your lifetime and that you are deliberately holding onto. Forgive yourself for those things in your past that you can no longer change and that result in a negative influence on your thinking. Forgive yourself for not being able to save the one you loved and lost to suicide. Forgiveness is necessary for sustaining health in all relationships. Let go, give it over to God, and be free from the "should haves," "could haves," and "what ifs" that trouble you.[26] Instead, forgive yourself for those mistakes and resolve to do better. All of these attitudes are a continual process.

> *To forgive is to set a prisoner free and to realize that prisoner was you.*
> —Lewis B. Smedes

The second is forgiveness of others. While confronting things that have happened in your past is painful and takes courage, it's important to reconcile with those who are present in your life and those you have lost even if there are legitimate reasons not to extend forgiveness to others. As Ira Byock has said, "This forgiveness is not about accepting or excusing; you may be entirely justified in hating the person; but hate keeps you chained to the person you despise." Forgiveness is for your own health and healing, not for the other person. Forgiveness, even though we may feel it's undeserved, is an important and vital expression of mercy.

When I was working at the hospital as a chaplain resident, I spent time with an adult patient who had been given only a

---

26 Byock, Ira. *The Four Things That Matter Most: A Book About Living*. New York: Free Press, 2004, pp. 70, 77.

short time to live. The patient had family around his bedside when I spoke to him regarding his end-of-life wishes. He insisted that his family contact his brother who he had been estranged from for over 30 years. His last wish was to reconcile with this brother. The family scrambled to make contact, since his brother lived out-of-state and arrangements would need to be made in order to get him there before the patient died. When I returned two days later, I learned that the brother had responded and they were reunited. He told me that a disagreement had kept them apart all those years, but the disagreement itself seemed insignificant at this pivotal time as he faced death.

No matter what the relationship between you and the person you lost, there are always regrets and questions that are painful and cause despair. Yet, with God's grace and the hope of our Lord Jesus Christ, we can heal from the pain of our past. If you seek forgiveness from the one you lost, even though you can no longer talk to them, you can still ask their forgiveness. Sometimes, those grieving feel guilt from the anger they feel, and it's the anger that needs to be expressed. No matter the emotions, it's important to recognize that harboring unforgiveness can be harmful because it will grow into bitterness, which will undermine your relationship with others and especially with God. The following are two examples of ways you can share forgiveness with the person you lost.

First, you can write a letter to that person and either express your remorse and ask their forgiveness or offer your forgiveness to them and share your emotions. Offer this letter to God in prayer. Some people destroy the letter after offering it to God, and others keep it. That's your choice. Second, you can find a room where you can be alone. As you sit in a chair, face an empty chair. Invite God to be present and claim this as a healing space by lighting a candle, reading a favorite Scripture, or offering a simple prayer. Imagine that the person you have lost is sitting there and, as you face them, have a conversation and share what's in your heart. Ask them for forgiveness and receive it. Offer your forgiveness and know they have received it. For closure, offer to God a prayer of gratitude and embrace God's peace and love as an affirmation of forgiveness and grace.

These examples are only two of many ways you can handle harmful negative emotions. In reconciling these matters with God, we heal those deep pockets of pain we have hidden away. Pain can be too much to bear on our own and can overwhelm us into despair. With God's tenderness, healing is possible.

> *Therefore....so that Jesus might be a merciful and faithful high priest in the service of God, to make a sacrifice of atonement for the sins of the people.*
> —Hebrews 2:17

**Embrace Mercy**

The Old Testament has many references to the assurance of God's mercy and reconciliation with God through sacrifice. The New Testament reveals the Good News of Redemption through Christ's sacrificial death on the cross. There are also Scriptures that remind us that, as individuals, we are to demonstrate mercy: *"Be merciful just as your Father is merciful"* (Luke 6:36). One way of demonstrating mercy as a chaplain is the ability to recognize another's deep pain and, without judgment but with compassion, assist them in recognizing the actions needed for resolution or reconciliation.

The parents of pediatric patients are often searching to make sense of their child's serious diagnosis of illness. In the midst of these situations, there have been times a parent would request a private visit to confess something from their past; oftentimes, it's a sin that they believe is unforgivable. In their anguish, they pour out their story. They tell me how they believe their child is ill because God is punishing them for this unconfessed sin. In this sacred space of confession, God's merciful forgiveness is sought through the assurance of Scripture and tearful prayers. *"Praise be to the Lord, for he has heard my cry for mercy."* (Psalm 28:6)

This illustration is significant as we realize God is always accessible and waiting for us to seek redemption. Recognition that harboring sin impacts our spiritual lives, we turn to the Lord's arms that are wide enough and deep enough to embrace us in forgiveness. By holding onto past sinfulness, we are allowing those sins a place in our spiritual hearts. There is no room for both sin and faithfulness to the Lord. One has to go, or we become a divided being instead of fully claiming the assurance of Christ's saving grace. Confession has a cleansing power that promotes healing and hope, and is a vitally essential spiritual discipline.

**Healing Practices**

Some examples of practical and healthy practices that further healing and hope in your grief process follow:

- Take a walk and sit in nature. Listen to the birds, watch the animals, and breathe deeply.

- Tour a flower garden and smell their fragrance, or buy a floral bouquet and place it in a prominent place in your home.

- Listen to music by going to a concert or surrounding yourself with music in your home.

- Go to the gym, run, ride a bike, or walk. Physical exercise is a great stress reliever, even when you are fatigued from your grief.

- Work outdoors in the garden or do yardwork.

- Practice meditation and yoga.

- Repeat or sing the following phrase: *Peace be still and know that I am God.* I liked to do this while power walking.

- Watch your favorite sports at an event or on TV.

- Pamper yourself with a massage and aromatherapy.

- Try drumming. If you don't have your own drum, borrow one, or find a group.

- Get a pet. Spend time walking the dog or playing with your cat.

- Take up hobbies and other activities that keep you engaged but allow you to relax.

- Spend time with children. Play with children by coloring, making playdough, racing toy cars. Or, hold an infant while rocking in a chair.

- Remember to breathe. Stop throughout the day and breathe in deeply and exhale deeply.

This is a short list to give you a starting point in your grief process. Design something uniquely for you and those you love.

> *To live is to suffer, to survive is to find some meaning in the suffering.*
> —Friedrich Nietzsche

**Wisdom Communities**

Throughout my life, I have been supported by delightful people, men and women who inspire and encourage me. These people form into small communities that provide hospitality, healing, and hope. Whatever the purpose of the group, whether casual or formal, they are welcoming and respectfully honor everyone's story. All groups serve uniquely different purposes but offer streams of wisdom throughout the conversations.

Of all the many small communities I have belonged to, I have found gatherings with women to be particularly warm and accepting. Flavorful stories are served up like generous slices of cake, and wisdom is gleaned as we savor the stories and linger over the discussion. The wisdom recipe is found in the shared experiences, stories of life and love that can encourage and reassure those around the table. Within a family or even a longtime group of friends, these stories are a great comfort because these people know you and have known you for much of your life. This acceptance, this sense of belonging, is like receiving a warm hug in a safe and sacred setting, where stories continue to be told and appreciated.

Spiritual gatherings such as Bible studies, minister meetings, or a group of neighbors who meet for coffee at their favorite eatery are settings where individuals acknowledge God's presence in their midst and designate it a sacred space, often over a prayer for the meal. This designation invites everyone to share their struggles and disappointments, dreams and successes. There is a spiritual wisdom that can be found in these conversations as Scripture may be reflected on, insights are discussed, and prayer concerns are shared. This wisdom is an intrinsic ingredient of the group that welcomes, inspires, and encourages, and is an important theme that has been a core aspect of all the groups that I have been a part of. The faces and settings have changed throughout the years, but all were influential in my personal and spiritual growth.

These sacred spaces were safe, because trust was established to allow a deeper level of sharing. Trust invited all to share their truth with an implicit assurance that confidentiality was key to the group as they discussed their own personal and spiritual struggles. Spiritual friendships are friends who value your vulnerability as you share your faith stories. As a group, they hold one another before God in prayer. Those meaningful relationships have walked with me through the many seasons of my life when I was growing up, married, a mother to babies who grew up to have their own families. These people were my community of wisdom and provided support for everyone in the group.

When I relocated and became a chaplain, I missed those gatherings and the central community of spiritual friends. So, I decided to form my own new community. Since reading was my favorite pastime, I chose to form a book club of women friends. I began by inviting new friends from the hospital community as well as my cousin who lived close by. For our first meeting, we selected a book to read as well as a date to begin. We met on the back porch of my little house, and each person brought a favorite dish to share for our meal. That was the beginning of our Back-Porch Book Club. Looking back on this group's formation, I can only say it was and continues to be an amazing community that has enriched my life, filled with women of faith and grace who share their wisdom, stories, doubts, and fears. Together, we rely on God for guidance and strength, and rely on each other for encouragement and support. Our book club started over eight years ago and has changed over the years as we now meet in a variety of locations. The faces have changed since we lost my cousin to cancer and then others moved to different parts of the country. What hasn't changed is the loving support we provide one another. This group was instrumental in my grief process, but even more, it provided a sacred space to share the doubts and discoveries of my faith. They held me in their prayers as I struggled with the intense suffering and shame of suicide loss. It was this group that encouraged me in my writing. The wisdom we share in our words and prayers has been and continues to be vital to our personal and spiritual growth.

One of the first places I was exposed to women's wisdom was within my own family community. At family gatherings for celebrations of birthdays, weddings, reunions, births, and deaths, women gather around the table and offer advice, often unsolicited, and gossip as we share all the news since we were last together. There is an interconnectedness felt that includes acceptance, encouragement, and most of all love. The wisdom of women and others of our community encourages us throughout our life. These nurturing relationships should be recognized and honored for their role in our lives.

Not everyone has a family to rely on for support, but there are others who surround us we can claim as family. My chaplain peers were very influential and supportive during my grief process. They acknowledged and respected my sorrow and were not uncomfortable walking with me through my dark times. With their encouragement and strength, I was able to face my doubts and despair, and finally reclaim my own strength. The chaplain community embraced me and provided a healing space where I discovered I wasn't the same person as I was before and would never be that person again. It is in the midst of suffering that shaping of the soul occurs. Suffering and sorrow reshaped and redefined me in ways that aren't always evident. As I sit in the Presence and experience the immeasurable love of God, I realize I am the closest to God in those moments. When I have used up all of my resources, everything that I have always relied upon within myself and within my community to get through life, it is there that I meet God. In my weakness, God becomes my strength. When I have nothing left to give, God gives to me. In the deepest darkness, God is my light. When I weep, God weeps with me. It is in that moment I realize I was never alone. *"The Lord is near."* (Philippians 4:5b)

**Reflections**

- Have you ever had to forgive yourself in order to forgive others? Is forgiveness a common practice for you? If not, what would it take for you to be more forgiving?

- Name a person or a group that has provided spiritual friendship for you, and recognize how they have enriched your life. If you don't have such a community, think about ways you can form such a community.

- In silence and solitude, read and reflect on Luke 10:27.

**Blessing**

*May Divine Love gentle your heart and spirit
with compassion and kindness.
Peace be still as you know and are assured
that God is present in all your times.*

# CHAPTER 11
## PATHWAY TO TRANSFORMATION

*Ministry After Suicide*

> …*I go out and heal others, even though I myself am not yet healed. I heal them through my brokenness, not through my power!*
> —Richard Rohr, *Simplicity*

When I returned to the children's hospital after the suicide, I recognized that my ministry would be influenced by my own grief process. By focusing on the needs of others, I discovered that through my own grief and sorrow, I intuitively connected with patients and families on a deeper level. It was also very healing as I focused on intentional ways to alleviate stress for families and to better engage in relationship with the patients.

By addressing the stress of the parents, particularly of the oncology moms, I realized from our conversations that their stress kept them from sleeping at night. The stress from their child's treatment as well as their isolation from family and friends during the long hospital visits kept them awake. In collaboration with these moms, we came up with several ideas to help with sleep, including hand-held labyrinths, mandalas, journals, and a tea cart that delivered cookies and beverages in the afternoon and encouraged social support. Since I was journaling through my own grief, I began making journals and included sample Scripture meditations. I purchased several yards of quilted fabric, hardback notebooks, and an exceptional permanent glue that you could spray on, and my back porch became my workroom. My first journal was a disaster, as I somehow managed to glue my fingers to the pages. Eventually, though, I developed a good method of assembly. It was a slow process, but I managed to produce one or two journals per night. This project was one of the best uses of my time as I focused on the needs of others instead of myself. For those who were spiritual, journaling the Scripture meditations was one way for them to process their anxiety and fears. Feedback from the parents was positive and encouraging.

Within a few months, I couldn't produce the journals fast enough. That's when I wrote my first grant request and received funding to continue the project. Several months later, two area churches had heard about my project and volunteered to assist by making the journals for me. In no time at all, I had more than enough journals to last for a year or more. Inspired by the journals, I developed a small inspiration and prayer booklet that our department had printed to give to patients and families throughout the hospital. That project was followed up by writing a children's booklet of faith activities for use in Christian and Jewish patient care.

My interactions with the patients became more focused on how to engage with them. During this time, I expanded my use of the colored stones and prompts about wondering with children. I also started telling stories with story figures and invited the children to retell the stories, provided mandalas for coloring, and handed out word searches that I had designed. Eventually, I put together a small bag to carry an assortment of journals, storybooks, figures, and colored stones.

End-of-life situations took on new meaning for me as I continually reviewed ways to include special readings, prayers, and rituals that offered comfort, some of which were designed specifically for the medical clinicians in end-of-life cases. Of course, there were organized group debriefings, but there was also a blessing of the room that allowed clinicians to acknowledge their sorrow for the deceased patient. This type of blessing had to be planned when the patient's room was empty and prior to another assigned patient's arrival. The clinicians were invited into the enclosed room, and a small candle was lit.

As prayers were offered, the clinicians were invited to share their reflections and feelings about the patient they cared for as well as their sorrow and loss. Acknowledgement of these feelings can be very healing and assists in bringing closure. Prayers of blessing were then offered for the clinicians, the room, and for the next patient to be received. Feedback has been very affirming of this type of blessing. Other ways to support medical staff was through a blessing of the hands of nurses. This sacred space involved recognition of the many ways nurses use their hands in serving others. A sweet-smelling oil was rubbed on their individual hands, and words of blessing and praise were given as an acknowledgement of their dedication.

By focusing on these and other initiatives, I was able to continue the path to process my own grief. I did not share my own story of grief but gentled my ministry to the patients, families and staff to connect with them at their most vulnerable moments by creating a sacred space in which to share their deepest thoughts and painful struggles.

There were other intrinsic ways I became more deeply involved in patient care, which are best described with an illustration. It's a story about how my heart and spirit were deeply impacted. On this particular day, I was paged to the Neonatal Intensive Care Unit, and upon arrival I noticed a very somber attitude among the staff. One nurse guided me to the patient, an extremely premature female infant. She had been flown in from a small town in another area of the state. She was born in an ambulance en route to the community hospital where her mother was admitted as a patient. The child was dying, and she was alone. The staff had called me so I could baptize and pray for her. After her baptism, I gently held her and rocked her. The nurses drew the privacy curtains around us; occasionally, one would check in to monitor her heartbeat. I softly sang to her, hummed familiar hymns, and told her how special she was to God. As I rocked, I cried. This continued for over an hour, and I'm certain I held her long after her heart stopped beating. It was difficult for me to return her to the nurses. What was a comfort was envisioning the Presence hovering over this child as I rocked, and then released her into the arms of Divine Love. This experience remains as vivid today as it was then. I can still envision her face and tiny body. This experience, among many others, greatly impacted and influenced my insights to the essence of death.

> *What does the Lord require of you but to do justice, and to love kindness, and to walk humbly with your God.*
> —Micah 6:8

### New Understandings

All our life experiences have the ability to shape, mold, and transform us in a variety of ways. There were two new understandings that I recognized had altered my perspective of God's benevolence. The first was the realization that my pediatric chaplaincy—the children, families, and staff—had become my new family. When I moved away from all I considered familiar, I thought I had lost my family by leaving my home and community behind to respond to God's call. In reality, I had gained a new family I could care for and love. That was a tremendous blessing.

Then there was a familiar quote from John C. Maxwell that I found buried among my papers: "Change is inevitable. Growth is optional." That's a choice for each individual. Our attitude and our response to life's changes and struggles often determine which path we choose. Those paths reflect either growth or resistance to growth. Growth is a lifelong process, and this list reflects some of my values at the present time.

- **Embrace more fully the spirit of adventure.** By being aware of and attentive for something more, something meaningful. I'm always ready to take on another project, another opportunity for learning, and to integrate and experience new spiritual disciplines.

    » Romans 12:2 *Do not be conformed to this world, but be transformed by the renewing of your minds, so that you may discern what is the will of God—what is good and acceptable and perfect.*

- **Resilience in my personal and spiritual life.** By remembering that God is my strength and always present in times of trouble, I trust that my devotional life will strengthen my center of peace that I continue to develop. I'm still working on being strong and remaining calm.

    » Joshua 1:9 *Be strong and courageous; do not be frightened or dismayed for the Lord your God is with you wherever you go.*

- **Appreciation and respect for life.** Understanding that we are all mortal and are not promised a tomorrow, I try to spend my time wisely and with purpose. Respect for life means we should do the best we can to make the most of every day and by purposeful living. Instead of fearing death, our thoughts instead reflect on the ways we can live out the Lord's call for compassionate action in our living. Respect your life and respect others. That doesn't mean living in denial of death but embracing life with an affirmation of purposeful living and loving.

> » Psalm 139:16b *In your book were written all the days that were formed for me, when none of them as yet existed.*

- **Love extravagantly.** Love your family and friends with a generous heart. Make time for hugs, birthdays, family gatherings, picnics, lunch with friends, and dates with your spouse or partner. Maintain those essential relationships by utilizing Dr. Ira Byock's valuable words: "Please forgive me; I forgive you; Thank you; and I love you."[27]

    > » 1 Corinthians 13:4–8 *Love is patient; love is kind; love is not envious or boastful or arrogant or rude. It does not insist on its own way; it is not irritable or resentful; it does not rejoice in wrongdoing, but rejoices in the truth. It bears all things, believes all things, hopes all things, endures all things. Love never ends.*

- **Be authentic and speak the truth.** To be authentic, we must begin to reclaim the truth about ourselves. Lies and secrets erode relationships and have a way of eventually

---

[27] Byock, Ira. *The Four Things That Matter Most: A Book About Living.* New York: Free Press, 2004, p. 3.

being revealed. Speak the truth whenever you can. We are all accountable for our words and actions without rationalizing, minimizing, or denying.

> » Ephesians 4:25 *So then, putting away falsehood, let all of us speak the truth to our neighbors, for we are members of one another.*

- **Worldview.** Instead of looking for the differences that divide us, I now look for the common ground that connects us as human beings, as God's creation. Diversity should not be a negative focus of our major differences. Instead, the emphasis should be on our uniquely distinguishable and distinctive attributes from one another. The Divine in me respects the Divine in thee.

> » Luke 10:27 *You shall love the Lord your God with all your heart, and with all your soul, and with all your strength, and with all your mind; and your neighbor as yourself.*

- **Humble in faith and in life. Demonstrate mercy and grace.** Recognizing that I'm a flawed human being, I'm more forgiving of myself and others. The pathway of forgiveness keeps me humble and grateful as I remain grounded in my faith.

> » 1 Peter 5:5–6 *And all of you must clothe yourselves with humility in your dealings with one another, for "God opposes the proud, but gives grace to the humble." Humble yourselves therefore under the mighty hand of God…*

## Pathway to Purposeful Giving

> *You are never too old to set another goal or to dream a new dream.*
> —C. S. Lewis

We all live with regrets. It's what we do with those regrets that makes a significant difference and influences our faith and life as well the lives of those around us. It is God's Divine Love, mercy, and grace that liberates us from the bondage of regret and invites us to a life of healing and hope. It's a path that calls to each of us as we discover there are many more things we can encounter and learn as we engage in adventure. As we all know, life means challenges as well as changes.

It was with great reluctance that I faced a change in my ministry. I felt as though I could no longer meet the needs of the patients, families, and staff because of my fatigue and physical limitations. Since I had met a wonderful man and remarried, my husband, Mark, encouraged me to retire. He was very supportive of my ministry but saw the toll it was taking on my health. It was very difficult for me to say goodbye to a ministry I embraced with passion and dedication.

Retirement was a new experience. I had the time to rest and recover, but I wondered: What do you do in retirement? That's when I prepared a list of goals. I needed something to focus on, a purpose for my days. I learned to swim and joined a gym. I planted an herb garden and expanded my cooking skills to use herbs in various recipes. I bought a French cookbook and learned how to cook with wine (bon appétit!). After one year of French cooking, which included lots of butter in the recipes, I had to stop because our waistlines expanded. I also bought a sewing machine and began some simple projects like pillowcases for the kiddos and table runners as gifts for family and friends. My husband loves to plan trips, and so now we have more flexibility to travel. And, of course, one of my main goals was to spend more time with family.

It only took one year of retirement to realize I needed to do something more meaningful. That's when I applied as a volunteer chaplain at UPMC Pinnacle Hospital in Harrisburg. After serving more than a year in one location, I was invited to serve at the Ortenzio Cancer Center, which I continue to this day. Sacred space as a chaplain continues to be that place where I sit with courageous and beautiful women and listen as they share their story. I'm honored and blessed to work with an amazing clinical staff who care for the women in this center. This assignment allows me to share my passion and experience as a hospital chaplain, and has helped me to discover that *purposeful giving* is vitally important for ourselves as well as the community we serve. Giving back generously of your time, skills, and abilities accumulated from a lifetime of experience is an affirmation of your life. It benefits the giver with purpose by providing the opportunity to develop meaningful relationships and a sense of belonging. Any organization you volunteer for benefits from the wisdom and experiences you share. Caring for others, no matter what capacity you are involved in, results in taking your eyes off yourself and focusing on the world around you. The unique gifts, wisdom, and life experiences we acquire are valuable assets that should be shared with others. Those intrinsic parts of your life can breathe life back to someone else as well as organizations and communities. The pathway to adventure is an awesome way to breathe life into your schedule and routine, especially in retirement. There is no age limit for growth and learning. Embracing adventure invites you to explore new possibilities in any season of life. You cannot fathom the wonders and the mysteries that lie beyond your horizon. Old dreams may become new possibilities, and new dreams may become realities as you seek something more for yourself.

Wonderings are still an important aspect of my spiritual life. In my reflections, I often return to the sacred space of my childhood and walk through the green pastures to follow a worn path to the gentle waters of a small stream. It is that place which calls to each of us to sit and rest awhile and to give ourselves permission to wonder. Your wonderings may be a search for God's love, mercy, and grace. It may be a search for peace out of the chaos, for forgiveness that weighs on your heart, or for significance and meaning of life. Whatever you are searching for, know that God awaits you.

Paradoxically, I now realize that in sharing my story, this book has become my sacred space. These are the unspoken words that I am now able to voice through writing. In this process, I have revealed facets of the deeply hidden sorrow that I struggle with yet, and the regrets, too painful to acknowledge, that I continue to relinquish into God's love. It is God's merciful forgiveness and Christ's redeeming grace that allows me to reclaim the memories of the past, because we cannot separate ourselves from our past. It's an integral part of who we are. Divine mercy has allowed me to forgive myself and others of those transgressions that oftentimes seem unpardonable and has allowed me to continue on this pathway of healing to hope. My prayer is that, with the eyes of your heart enlightened, you may allow your mind, your inner awareness, and your spirit to encounter Divine Love, mercy, and grace. May it be so.

## Reflections

- Reflect on the "Four Things That Matter Most" by Dr. Byock: *Please forgive me, I forgive you, Thank you, I love you.* Journal ways you can integrate them more fully for hope and healing in your relationships.

- Identify the values that guide your everyday living. Identify one value or priority that you would like to further develop in your life.

- Consider what it means to purposefully give back and identify those skills and abilities that you could share. Seriously consider the places where you can share your wealth of experience.

## Blessing

*May your Sacred Space
embrace you with Divine Love,
the richness of God's mercy and
the grace of our Lord Jesus Christ.
Amen.*

# Acknowledgements

There are many people I consider my *beloved* who I extend heartfelt gratitude toward.

First and foremost, my very special thanks and much love to my husband, Mark, for his encouragement and enduring patience as I spent hours writing. Among others to thank are my family. My mom, dad, sisters, and brother as well as their spouses have accompanied and supported me in all the times of my life. They provided love when I felt unlovable and support when I was feeling alone.

Much love to my beautiful daughters, Kelli and Jodi, who are brave and courageous wives and mothers as they demonstrate extravagant love in nurturing their own families. And appreciation to Kirby and Jon for being loving husbands and fathers. To Jaysen and Christina, loving thanks for your encouragement and support. Hugs and love to my grandchildren, who continue to demonstrate wonder and joy in everything they experience.

Many thanks to the community of women friends who have accompanied, nurtured, and supported me in my faith journey. Special recognition belongs to my book club friends as they encouraged me in the writing of this book and were part of the beta editors' group. Thank you, Ann, Julie, and Marie for your spiritual friendship and prayers. We have greatly missed our friend Tootie, and we still hear her words, "It's all good!" It is to my cousin and friend that I dedicate this writing as well as to all chaplains who respond to God's call to this vital ministry.

Very special thanks to Rev. Paul Derrickson and Rev. Angelina Van Hise for your supervision during my Clinical Pastoral Education as well as being valued colleagues and friends. Words cannot express the gratitude I have for your many kindnesses and encouragement.

Thank you to my chaplain peers at Penn State Hershey Medical Center. Your peer support, encouragement, and love were greatly appreciated. You do amazing work every day, and I feel honored to have served among you and greatly value our enduring friendship.

The Pediatric Chaplains Network supports and encourages the professional growth and continued research of children's spirituality. Many thanks for your peer support over the years.

My sincere thanks to Rev. Elizabeth Bidgood Enders and Rev. Greg Bidgood Enders for your assistance as beta readers and in recognition of and respect for the various ministries you provide to your church and community.

Special thanks to Morgan Gist MacDonald of Paper Raven Books and her amazing publishing team for assistance in making this book a reality.

# BIBLIOGRAPHY

Bonhoeffer, Dietrich. *The Cost of Discipleship.* New York: Touchstone Press, 1959.

Byock, Ira. *The Four Things That Matter Most: A Book About Living.* New York: Free Press, 2004.

Calhoun, Adele Ahlberg. *Spiritual Disciplines Handbook: Practices That Transform Us.* Downers Grove, IL: InterVarsity Press, 2005.

Clarke, Lowther W. K., *A Pax Book.* London: SPCK Publishing, 1931. http://www.solesmes.com/sites/default/files/upload/pdf/rule_of_st_benedict.pdf.

de Waal, Esther. *Seeking God: The Way of St. Benedict.* Collegeville, MN: Liturgical Press, 1984.

Farnham, Suzanne G., Gill, Joseph P., McLean, R. Taylor, Ward, Susan M. *Listening Hearts: Discerning Call in Community.* Harrisburg, PA: Morehouse Publishing, 1991.

Hart, Tobin. *The Secret Spiritual World of Children: The Breakthrough Discovery that Profoundly Alters Our Conventional View of Children's Mystical Experiences.* Maui, HI: Inner Ocean Publishing, 2003.

Heschel, Abraham Joshua. *God In Search of Man: A Philosophy of Judaism.* New York: Farrar, Straus and Giroux, 1955.

Kavanaugh, Kieran, Rodriguez, Otilio. *The Collected Works of St. John of the Cross.* Washington, DC: ICS Publications, 1991.

National Institute of Mental Health. "Suicide." May 2018. www.nimh.nih.gov/health/statistics/suicide.shtml.

Newhouse, Meg. "Legacy: A Powerful Rite of Passage." *Social Network Today* 10, no. 3 (May/June 2010): 6.

Nouwen, Henri J. M., Christensen, Michael J., Lair, Rebecca J. *Discernment: Reading the Signs of Daily Life*. New York: HarperCollins, 2013.

Nouwen, Henri J. M. *Spiritual Direction: Wisdom for the Long Walk of Faith*. New York: HarperCollins, 2006.

———. *The Way of The Heart: Connecting with God Through Prayer, Wisdom, and Silence*. New York: Ballantine Books, 1981.

Rohr, Richard. *Simplicity: The Freedom of Letting Go*. New York: The Crossroad Publishing Company, 2003.

Serani, Deborah. "Understanding Survivors of Suicide Loss—Suicide is a Death Like No Other." *Psychology Today*, Nov. 25, 2013. www.psychologytoday.com/us/blog/two-takes-depression/201311/understanding-survivors-suicide-loss.

Smedes, Lewis. "Is Suicide Unforgivable?" *Christianity Today*, July 10, 2000. www.christianitytoday.com/ct/2000/July10/30.61.html.

Substance Abuse and Mental Health Services Administration. US Department of Health and Human Services. http://www.samhsa.gov.

Suicide Prevention Resource Center. "About Suicide." 2016. www.sprc.org/about-suicide.

———. "The Role of Faith Communities in Preventing Suicide: A Report of an Interfaith Suicide Prevention Dialogue." Newton, MA: Education Development Center, Inc., 2009. http://www.sprc.org/sites/default/files/migrate/library/faith_dialogue.pdf.

Survivors of Suicide Loss Task Force. "Responding to Grief, Trauma, and Distress After a Suicide: U.S. National Guidelines." National Action Alliance for Suicide Prevention. April 2015. https://www.sprc.org/sites/default/files/migrate/library/RespondingAfterSuicideNationalGuidelines.pdf.

Walker, Matthew. *Adventure in Everything: How the Five Elements of Adventure Create a Life of Authenticity, Purpose, and Inspiration.* New York: Hay House, Inc., 2011.

White, James R. *Grieving: Your Path Back to Peace.* Minneapolis: Bethany House Publishers, 1997.

Young, Ilanit Tal, Iglewicz, Alana, Glorioso, Danielle, Lanouette, Nicole, Seay, Kathryn, Ilapakurti, Manjusha, Zisook, Sidney. "Suicide Bereavement and Complicated Grief." *Dialogues in Clinical Neuroscience* 14, no. 2 (2012).

# Suicide & Grief Resources

If you or someone you know is in need of help, call the National Suicide Prevention Lifeline:
1-800-273-TALK (8255)

Provides access to trained telephone counselors, 24 hours a day, 7 days a week.

Or contact the Crisis Text Line by texting TALK to 741741.


AAS—American Association of Suicidology
202-237-2280
www.suicidology.org

AFSP—American Foundation for Suicide Prevention
1-888-333-AFSP (2377)
www.afsp.org

Alliance of Hope
847-868-3313
www.allianceofhope.org

Friends for Survival
916-392-0664
www.friendsforsurvival.org

Heartbeat—Grief Support Following Suicide
www.heartbeatsurvivorsaftersuicide.org

LOSSteam—Local Outreach to Suicide Survivors
www.lossteam.com

Mental Health America
703-684-7722
www.mentalhealthamerica.net

National Action Alliance for Suicide Prevention
202-572-3784
www.actionallianceforsuicideprevention.org

Pennsylvania Suicide Prevention Coalition
717-885-9161
www.PreventSuicidePA.org

Sources of Strength
https://sourcesofstrength.org

SPRC—Suicide Prevention Resource Center
1-877-438-7772
www.sprc.org

SPTS USA—Society for the Prevention of Teen Suicide
732-410-7900
www.sptsusa.org

Stop a Suicide Today
www.stopasuicide.org

The Compassionate Friends
877-969-0010
www.compassionatefriends.org

The Jason Foundation—Prevention of youth suicide
1-888-881-2323
www.jasonfoundation.org

The Jed Foundation—Suicide prevention for college students
212-647-7544
www.jedfoundation.org

The Link's National Resource Center for Suicide Prevention and Aftercare
404-256-2919
linknrc@thelink.org
www.thelink.org

The Trevor Project—Suicide prevention for the LGBT community
866-488-7396
www.thetrevorproject.org

Veterans Crisis Line
1-800-273-8255 (x1) or send a text to 838255
www.veteranscrisisline.net

VETS4Warriors
855-838-8255
www.vets4warriors.com
vets4warriors@ubhc.rutgers.edu

Yellow Ribbon Suicide Prevention Program
303-429-3530
www.yellowribbon.org

# Additional Resources

Bass, Dorothy C. *Receiving the Day.* San Francisco: Jossey-Bass, 2000.

Bolton, Iris with Mitchell, Curtis. *My Son…My Son…A Guide to Healing After Death, Loss or Suicide.* Buford, GA: Bolton Press Atlanta, 1983.

Bolton, Iris. *Voices of Healing and Hope: Conversations on Grief after Suicide.* Buford, GA: Bolton Press Atlanta, 2017.

Bozarth, Alla Renee. *Life Is Goodbye, Life Is Hello.* Center City, MN: Hazelden Foundation, 1994.

Hall, Thelma, R. C. *Too Deep for Words: Rediscovering Lectio Divina.* New York: Paulist Press, 1988.

Noel, Brook and Blair, Pamela D. *I Wasn't Ready to Say Goodbye: Surviving, Coping, and Healing After the Sudden Death of a Loved One.* Naperville, IL: Sourcebooks, Inc., 2000.

Richardson, Jan L. *In the Sanctuary of Women: A Companion for Reflection and Prayer.* Nashville, TN: Upper Room Books, 2010.

Rupp, Joyce. *Praying Our Goodbyes.* Notre Dame, IN: Ave Maria Press, 1988.

Wicks, Robert J. *Living A Gentle, Passionate Life.* Mahwah, NJ: Paulist Press, 1998.

———. *Perspective: The Calm Within the Storm.* New York: Oxford University Press, 2014.

**Grief Books for Children**

Bernardo, Susan. Fletcher, Courtenay, Illustrator. *Sun Kisses, Moon Hugs.* Los Angeles: Inner Flower Child Book, 2012.

Holmes, Margaret M. Pillo, Cary, Illustrator. *A Terrible Thing Happened.* Washington, DC: Magination Press, 2000.

Olivieri, Laura. Elder, Kristin, Illustrator. *Where Are You? A Child's Book about Loss.* Lulu, 2007.

Rowland, Joanna. Baker, Thea, Illustrator. *The Memory Box: A Book About Grief.* Minneapolis: Sparkhouse Family, 2017.

Schwiebert, Pat, and DeKlyen, Chuck. Bills, Taylor, Illustrator. *Tear Soup: A Recipe For Healing After Loss.* Vancouver, WA: Grief Watch, 1999.

www.ingramcontent.com/pod-product-compliance
Lightning Source LLC
Chambersburg PA
CBHW030636150426
42811CB00077B/2180/J